The Sea People

A Captivating Guide to the Seafarers Who Invaded Ancient Egypt, Eastern Anatolia, the Hittite Empire, Palestine, Syria, and Cyprus, along with the Late Bronze Age Collapse

Free Bonus from Captivating History (Available for a Limited time)

Hi History Lovers!

Now you have a chance to join our exclusive history list so you can get your first history ebook for free as well as discounts and a potential to get more history books for free! Simply visit the link below to join.

Captivatinghistory.com/ebook

Also, make sure to follow us on Facebook, Twitter and Youtube by searching for Captivating History.

Table of Contents

Introduction

Greece is a wonderful place to go on vacation. It offers beautiful beaches, incredible history, and delicious food for tourists. The history dates back over 4,000 years and is fascinating everywhere. Many of the most popular sites existed before the common era.

Mycenae is a popular visiting destination. Less than fifty miles southwest of Athens, Mycenae was one of the eastern Mediterranean's principal centers of power in the Bronze Age. A dominating symbol of the might of the ancient city is the Lion Gate. It stands 3.10 meters wide and 2.95 meters high at its threshold. The magnificent entrance with its two lions represents the power and the might of the rulers and the respect given to the city by all the people who lived in the Aegean area. Visitors will stop to stare and take pictures at the Lion Gate, but only an experienced archaeology professional's eyes will notice something is wrong.

The fault can be found in the lower portion of the right-hand pillar of the gate. The post is partially damaged, and there are significant flaws in the masonry and the sculpture relief of the lion, which adorns the pillar. A volcano or an earthquake did not do damage to the pillar. It was the work of man and, more specifically, a large group of men trying to force their way into the city. The cracked masonry is testimony to a force that rocked Late Bronze Age civilizations to their core.

It is believed that this was the work of the Sea People—the scourge of the eastern Mediterranean in the 13th and 12th centuries BCE. The attack on Mycenae was not an isolated event. The Sea People ranged all over the Aegean Sea, and there is evidence of their path of destruction in Greece, Egypt, and Asia Minor. The Sea People were a force to be reckoned with and a wrecking crew that struck fear and terror into the hearts of the low and the mighty. The exploits of these seafaring marauders are recorded in the official records of the Egyptians, ancient Greeks, and Hittites. Their barbarism is credited with bringing the downfall of two major powers of antiquity.

Who were these people? Where did they come from, and what did they have that made them so successful in their raids? They are a historical riddle that has fascinated historians and archaeologists for centuries. Unfortunately, the Sea People did not leave behind libraries of official records, and there is no evidence of sophisticated culture or innovative art to suggest they were significant contributors to the society of the era. All that is presently known is that they were raiders and effective plunderers.

The Sea People are also a topic of numerous conversations regarding the Late Bronze Age in Europe and the Middle East. The more we know about them, the more we can understand forces that brought on significant instability and chaos in the final years of a historical age. They are an enticing subject that is worth examining.

Knowing the Sea People is what this book is all about. We will do more than mention the hammer blows they dealt to civilizations three thousand years ago. We will look at the information we have about this group of marauders and investigate what motivated them and how they changed once-stable communities and countries. We will also suggest along the way that an interesting piece of ancient history might have been the consequence of what the Sea People did.

History can be tedious if it is nothing but battles that were fought or the destruction people wrought. We know that the Sea People engaged in large-scale destruction, but what were their intentions beyond burning things down? We will discuss matters such as commercial interests, cultural inclinations, and how the Sea People may have fit into the foreign policy of the Late Bronze Age. These sea rovers left behind a legacy, and we are going to investigate it. The Late Bronze Age was a time of significant change. Some of those historical developments will be examined, and if there are any lessons worth learning, we will discuss them in this book.

The builders of civilization always receive our attention. Those that destroy cultures ordinarily get a passing reference. Undoubtedly, the Sea People were a devastating power in the eastern Mediterranean, and we intend to look at more than a few instances. The extent of their impact is essential to understanding the final days of the Bronze Age. We will cover this as we follow along the path the Sea People left behind.

Chapter 1 – The Origins

The Late Bronze Age has been described as the worst disaster in ancient history. Chaos gradually took over from civilized order marking the end of the Hittite Empire, Kassites, Mycenaean states, Ugarit, and the Amorite kingdoms. Some cultures did survive this time, but they were severely damaged and could not restore the majesty and power they previously held. The Sea People were among the agents of change.

Where they came from remains a mystery, but there are several theories about their origin. Some places that nurtured the original pirates include Western Asia Minor, the Aegean, Mediterranean islands off the coast of Greece, and possibly southern Europe. French Egyptologist Emmanuel de Rouge coined the phrase "peoples de la mer," or "Sea People," to give a name to them.

The Possible Ancestors

We are handicapped in our search because the Sea People did not leave behind written records. Egyptian accounts give us a clue about where the Sea People came from. The ancient texts suggest the cultures that spawned the Sea People might have been the Sherden, Denyen, Ekwesh, Lukka, Peleset, Shekelesh, Teresh, Tjekker, and Weshesh. Other possibilities include the Etruscans, Trojans, Philistines, Mycenaeans, or even what was left of Minoan society (Milligan, 2020).

The Sherden were the most famous of the Sea People and were distinguished by distinctive horned helmets. The Egyptians recognized their ability as fighters, and Ramesses II had a guard unit comprised of Sherden warriors. The Shekelesh can be identified in Egyptian reliefs by their bronze skullcaps and habit of carrying no shield.

The Peleset can be identified in reliefs by the feathered tiaras they wore. Peleset were taken prisoner by the Egyptians after the battle of Zahi, settled in the northeastern area of Egypt, and are associated with the Philistines of the Bible (Doherty, 2022).

The Lukka, another major group, might not have been pirates originally but were forced into that trade through necessity. The Lukka probably originated in southwestern Turkey in the Lycia region.

The Denyen and the Ekwesh might be from the Aegean and correspond to the Danaans and Achaeans mentioned in Homer's *Iliad*. Other Sea People tribes may have had contact with Troy, and it has been proposed that the Tjekker, Weshesh, and the Teresh were refugees from the Trojan War. The Teresh could have been related to the Tyrsensians, after whom the Tyrrhenian Sea is named.

An interesting possibility of where some of the tribes might have come from is gleaned from linguistic studies. Egyptian sources mention people known as the Sherden, who came from Shardana. There is a word link between Shardana and Sardinia. There are also linguistic similarities between the Shekelesh and Sicily. This means the Sea People may have started from the Western Mediterranean and moved eastward. They were not an ethnic group, per se, but an assortment of various tribes or cultures. As they moved eastward, the Sea People may have gathered recruits interested in looting.

Archaeologists keep looking for clues, and a Philistine cemetery discovered at the site of Ashkelon in Israel may provide some information. DNA analysis of the skeletons could identify if the deceased trace their ancestry to the Aegean or the Western Mediterranean (Cline, 2016).

What Motivated the Sea People?

Piracy is one of the world's oldest professions, and any landmass with a seacoast is vulnerable to looting expeditions. What makes the Sea People unique is the size and scope of their attacks on their victims. It was more than just one or two raiding vessels and could be sizable fleets.

What motivated the Sea People to take to the water and commit piracy? There may have been several significant reasons for taking such extreme action against their neighbors.

Environmental change might have played a role. A recent study published in the scientific journal *Nature* discusses the possibility that the Hittites were forced to endure consecutive years of a devastating drought that made it difficult to grow food crops and caused large-scale famines. Evidence was found in the tree rings of recently excavated juniper wood. Research showed rings of the juniper wood had unusually low growth for several years. Scientists believe this evidence of a lack of rain and a subsequent devastating drought was particularly noticeable between 1198 and 1196 BCE. Those conditions would have created catastrophic food supply disruption and exacerbated social problems. Desperate people will take desperate actions, and the crop failures over a period of years may have forced various groups to acts of piracy (Tigue, 2023).

Climate changes could have had a domino effect. Drought and famine could easily create economic disruption. Taxes based on crop yields would've fallen drastically, and money ordinarily allocated for coastal defenses was not there. Internal dissension could have led to power vacuums that allowed pirate fleets to operate with impunity, knowing there would be no noticeable resistance from central authorities. Not being able to thwart the Sea People caused the downfall of numerous political regimes. The collapse would include what were once major power centers.

Social instability is also a factor that cannot be ignored. It would have been more than just class warfare or rebellions. Mass migrations of people would have caused considerable strain on already depleted resources, forcing seaports to absorb large groups of economic refugees. We know from archaeological findings that during the reign of Ramses III (1186 to 1155 BCE), tomb robbing, something unthinkable in earlier years, was becoming widespread. The researchers discovered that the items stolen from the graves were not always gold or jewels; food was a significant item for thieves (O'Reilly, 2022).

The Sea People were in the middle of significant disruption and turmoil, and chaos created opportunities to be exploited. We cannot discount the chance that piracy was a way of life for some of these ethnic groups. Indeed, some of the Sea People may have been well-versed in naval plunder, and the disorder caused by climate change, famine, internal disruption, and political instability provided the opportunity to use already well-honed skills.

Technological Superiority

A reason for the success of the Vikings in the Middle Ages was the superior design of their fighting ships. These were shaped for speed and could move in relatively shallow inland rivers. Likewise, the Sea People may have been able to take advantage of advances in Bronze Age maritime technology.

A significant advance was the invention of the brailed rig and loose-footed square sail. Before this development, sailors relied on large square sails held fast by upper and lower yards. Boats with large sails were an improvement over those that were propelled only by oars. However, the large square sail was primarily effective for downwind travel, and the maneuverability was limited. The brailed rig and loose-footed square sail had lines attached to the bottom that were run vertically through rings sewn to the front of the sail, then run over to the yard and the stern. This meant it could be easily raised, lowered, and manipulated like a Venetian blind. The loose-footed sail offered excellent maneuverability and could sail much closer to the wind.

This innovation, combined with Helladic oared rowing, resulted in a break with earlier ship design and significantly advanced naval activity. The sail allowed the rowing crew a chance to rest and provided the opportunity to sail in nearly every direction. The Helladic oared galley, with banks of rowers, added to the ship's speed. Helladic oared galleys with brailed rigs and loose-footed square sails were ideal for piracy (Emanuel, 2014).

These ships fit in nicely with the tactics employed by the Sea People. The fast-moving vessels were ideal for surprise attacks on unsuspecting targets. The ships permitted them to perform what amounted to smash-and-grab robberies: they could strike quickly and withdraw before their victims could launch a counterattack. (These raids were ordinarily initiated under cover of darkness or in bad weather.) Moreover, the speed and maneuverability of the galleys permitted these raiders to go from one location to another, making it difficult for their enemies to mount an effective defense.

The Sea People exhibited a willingness to take risks. Raiding parties would have been smaller than the forces that enemies could produce, but this was not a disadvantage. Sea People wanted fast strikes and large profits. It does not appear they were willing to fight major battles unless it was necessary. Consequently, their losses were small, and the benefits derived from an attack were enormous.

A final consideration is that no one could predict where the Sea People would strike. However, they were flexible enough in their strategies to avoid the strong points and exploit the weaknesses of any coastal region. It added to their success and heightened the fear of those exposed to their lightning raids.

Weapons and Armor

There is no evidence the Sea People used iron weapons. What we know suggests that they used spears, long swords, axes, and bows and arrows. The reliefs found on the memorial temple at Medinet Habu display highly functional armor that was very flexible. The evidence indicates that their weapon technology was superior to what was commonly used. However, it probably did not matter. What the Sea People had was maritime speed and maneuverability. It was easy to get in and out quickly, so they did not have to engage in prolonged combat.

Scholars speculate that the Sea People were a confederacy of various groups. They probably coordinated their raids so that one did not conflict with the objectives of another. If so, they could, on occasion, quickly mobilize large forces that would easily overwhelm weaker opponents.

One element of surprise was clearly their novelty. The eastern Mediterranean had never dealt with something like the Sea People before. Land raids were understandable because they were the usual means of attacking economic targets. Groups of galleys operating as a strike force were previously unknown, and defense systems were not equipped to deal with maritime surprises. Moreover, the Sea People had an advantage in that they could employ all their martial resources optimally. For a time, they were almost unstoppable.

Bronze Age kingdoms prospered through trade and innovative changes in commerce. Unfortunately, these same monarchies offered numerous opportunities for pillage. They demonstrated vulnerabilities that they might have ignored but others did not. All it would take was superior technology, a clever strategy, and the ability to size up a prospective victim. The Sea People had the resources and the cunning to exploit whatever chance came their way. Established trade routes and power centers became lucrative targets. Not even the mightiest states of the age were immune to sea raids. These pillaging expeditions became frequent occurrences as the Sea People better understood their targets.

The Bronze Age culture of the eastern Mediterranean emphasized trade and the blossoming of culture through poetry and the arts. It was a time when humanity was making significant progress in many fields. The area could be likened to a garden where civilization was flowering, and everyone was as busy as bees working toward significant achievements and pollinating the world with incredible innovations. The Sea People were army ants in this beautiful image of an ever-improving social ecosphere. It was a time when a reasonably stable corner of the world suddenly was pitched into a cataclysm the inhabitants could barely understand or successfully confront.

Chapter 2 – The Groups Within the Sea People

We have mentioned the tribes that comprised the Sea People, and now we will go into more detail about their cultures and ethnicities. The Sea People were not a distinct demographic group. They came from different areas and had customs that were unique to them. Combined into a confederacy, they were a frightening force in the Late Bronze Age and changed the course of history.

Sherden

We first learn about the Sherden in the records of the Egyptian Pharaoh Rameses II, who fought them in a naval battle and defeated them. Interestingly, the pharaoh made use of those whom he captured. They became part of the bodyguard and were depicted in reliefs as wearing helmets with horns and a ball projecting from the middle. Their round shields and great swords also made them stand out. The Pharaoh noted in the records that Sherden warriors were part of the personal bodyguard at the battle of Kadesh.

The Sherden were seafaring people who specialized in maritime trade. They were considered skilled navigators and shipbuilders and were able to establish trade networks in the eastern Mediterranean. They were also involved in piracy and organized warrior bands whose members were renowned for courage and ferocity in battle.

The Sherden's reputation as fierce warriors led to them being hired as mercenaries throughout the eastern Mediterranean. This provides a clue to their success. As bodyguards to the pharaoh, they were probably familiar with the Egyptian army's military organization and battle tactics. Their mercenary status no doubt acquainted them with the military capabilities of other countries in the area, giving them inside knowledge that would prove helpful in sea raiding efforts (Wikipedia.org, 2023).

Peleset

The earliest reference to the Peleset comes from the Medinet Habu temple of Egypt. They are depicted as an enemy of Ramesses III in the Battle of the Delta. They settled in the southern coastal area of Canaan after their defeat. The area where they settled was known as Philistia, and they are referred to as the Philistines in the Bible. They were known for having a highly organized military hierarchy, including chariots, infantry, and archers. Like the Sherden, the Peleset were employed as mercenaries in the region.

Notably, the Peleset culture was a mixture of Aegean, Canaanite, and Egyptian elements. They worshiped a pantheon of deities, including the goddess Astarte and the god Dagon. The Peleset had distinctive pottery, which they decorated with geometric patterns and animal motifs.

Shekelesh

Pharaoh Merneptah left an account of how he defeated the Shekelesh in a naval battle. These people may have come from as far west as the Balearic Islands and were recognized by a distinctive round shield and their use of spears and slingshots. While they were best known for their naval activity, they also fought on land as mercenaries.

Ekwesh

Their place of origin in western Anatolia suggests they were familiar with the Hittite Empire, how it was governed, and how the Hittites fought. The Ekwesh had helmets adorned with horns or crests and used shields and body armor made of either leather or metal. Although some of them might have settled in the region of Canaan, it is also possible that the Ekwesh migrated to other parts of the Mediterranean where they would continue seagoing activities.

We have sparse information about the religion of the Ekwesh, but they may have worshipped the gods and goddesses of the Canaanite and Hittite pantheons. Their beliefs were probably in a polytheistic religion with animal sacrifices and other rituals. The Ekwesh might also have worshipped natural phenomena, such as the sea or the sun, which were essential elements of this seafaring culture.

Several of the Sea People groups are associated with the Achaeans. If so, the Ekwesh might have played a role in the Homeric history and legends surrounding the city of Troy.

Denyen

The archives of the Hittite Empire are the primary source for this group of the Sea People. They were described by the Hittites as allies of the Ahhiyawa. They were among the Sea People who were defeated in battle by Ramesses III.

It is believed that some of them may have settled in Canaan, which is the basis of an interesting theory about the Denyen. An Israeli archaeologist, Yigael Yadin, has proposed that the Denyen were linked to the Israelite tribe of Dan. This is the cause of some heated discussions among archaeologists who dispute the use of the Bible as a credible source.

An interesting reference in the fourth and fifth chapters of the book of Judges concerns the war Deborah and Barack fought with Jabin, the king of Canaan. Deborah and Barak wanted to unite all Israelite forces under one banner, but not all the tribes of Israel responded to their request. Judges 5:17 contains this interesting phrase:

"Why did Dan remain in ships?"

The tribe of Dan was possibly a seafaring tribe with interests outside of Israel. The word "remain" might indicate that Dan's preoccupation with the ocean was already well-established. We already know that Israel was heavily involved in maritime trade. The tribe of Dan may have been the Denyen, and this group of people may have been heavily involved in maritime commerce. The name similarity possibly shows that Dan and Denyen are one and the same (Mckoy, 2022).

Lukka

The Lukka came from the Lukka region of Anatolia and were part of a minor Hittite state, Arzawa. It appears there is no primary political importance to these people and no evidence of a Lukka king, but they were probably expert seafarers. Their raiding involvement would have included not only attacks along the coast but also land-based attacks into the interior of Anatolia.

The Lukka took part in an attack on Egypt led by Libyan tribes. What is noteworthy about the incursion is that families accompanied the warriors on this excursion. This suggests that the Lukka were not primarily interested in seizing as much booty as possible. Instead, they may have been intent on settling down in that region (History Files, 2023).

Tjekker

This group came from somewhere in the Aegean Islands, and there is evidence they settled in Canaan. Excavations at Tel Dor in Israel point to a city known as Tjekker. It was large and well-fortified and was destroyed in the 11th century BCE. It was a case where the hunter became the game—a city of the Sea People that was ultimately destroyed, probably by the Phoenicians (The Univesity of Chicago Press Journals, 2023).

A puzzle involving the Tjekker is the reason for their settling in Canaan. These people were primarily from the Anatolia area, so why were they settling in Canaan, and, more importantly, why were these sea raiders tolerated? An answer may lie in Egyptian foreign policy. Caravan routes were immensely important to the economy of Egypt. However, attacks from nomads continually threatened the overland trade routes. Therefore, the Egyptians may have promoted the settlement of Sea People, such as the Tjekker in Canaan, to protect the commercial interests of Egypt.

Wesheh

These are the least known of the Sea People. They are only mentioned in documents from the reign of Ramesses III, and there is no visual representation of them. There are some phonetic similarities between the Weshesh and others who lived in Asia Minor and Crete, but those fragments of information are all we have.

Communication

The fact that the Sea People were a confederacy of various ethnic groups raises the question of how they could communicate with each other. Those from Sardinia probably had a mother tongue different from those in western Anatolia or Cyprus. There must have been some way for these diverse groups to spread messages and share information.

One possibility is that the Sea People used gestures and sign language to communicate with each other, especially during naval raids. Unspoken communication may have been standardized throughout the various groups and have permitted them to overcome any language difficulties. Flags are a typical means of communication between ships at sea. Those flags may have been used as cloth messages and to identify ships as Sea People vessels.

Research suggests that a common language among several Sea People groups was present. Lukka was a base for the Sea People in Southwest Anatolia, and this region is where several Sea People came from. Luwian is the patois of the area, and it is possible that many Sea People either knew the language or were familiar with key phrases.

There might have even been a written Sea People language based on the Luwian script. For example, a stele discovered in 1878 is written in Luwian text, and it tells of the Sea People. Some scholars claim this is a key to how the Sea People communicated, but this theory requires more corroboration before it is accepted as genuine (Panko, 2017).

A final explanation could be the extensive interaction between the various groups. Sea People were hired as mercenaries by many different nations. Sea People ethnicities were intermingled among the employers. By close interaction, they may have become familiar with enough words from each other's languages to explain what they wanted to do. As a result, a form of pidgin language, combining phrases from several groups, may have evolved. Speculation continues, but it is evident that the Sea People found a way to talk to each other and plan naval invasions.

Coordination of Activity

Credit has to be given to these sea marauders for their effectiveness at striking areas without warning. Moreover, it does not appear that the raids overlapped with each other. The Sea People somehow coordinated activities in a way that allowed everybody to get a piece of the action.

There must have been some sort of planning before the attacks were made. For example, a ship belonging to one of the Sea People groups might have been able to disguise itself and scout the coast, looking for vulnerable opportunities. Trade involved the constant collection and dispersal of intelligence. In the ordinary course of doing business, Sea People may have been made aware of a war or some internal discord that created an opportunity to strike. Yet there is still the question of how they made lightning moves against their unsuspecting prey.

A neural center of this confederacy may have disseminated information and helped plan various attacks. It might have been a port controlled by the Sea People, where delegates would meet and review the situations. (An idea of what might've been a logical locus of planning will be discussed later in this book.)

The confederacy might also have been analogous to Mafia families in the United States. They may have agreed that certain parts of the eastern Mediterranean would be assigned to a given group. That would prevent internal rivalries from getting out of hand and allow everybody to profit from piracy.

How they coordinated activity is a field of exciting speculation, and we will learn more about this as archaeology uncovers the secrets. However, we can confidently say that the Sea People were not a bunch of rowdy buccaneers. They seem to have been a Late Bronze Age association with a business plan for pillage and mayhem. The evidence is overwhelming that they were not serendipitously striking trade centers along the coast of Anatolia, Egypt, and the Levant. The Sea People knew what they were doing.

Chapter 3 – Sea People Records

What they accomplished was the stuff of legends, but the Sea People were not myths. They were real, and we have evidence and corroborating information to paint a picture of a terror of the waters in the Late Bronze Age. Whether told through reliefs carved into the wall of the temple or clay tablets baked in a kiln and then archived, the story of the Sea People is not a complete mystery and definitely not a work of fiction. What makes the information solid is that there are several major and minor sources of evidence about the Sea People, and they can be found in various areas in the eastern Mediterranean. The major powers in the Aegean Sea were very aware of what these marauders could do and what the Sea People did to their victims.

The Hittite Archives

Unlike the Mycenaeans, the Hittites have extensive records and documentation of daily life and official activities. Libraries of tablets contain stories written in cuneiform that provide us with source material. Those libraries are in addition to monumental reliefs scattered throughout the Hittite region. The archaeological dig at Karatepe includes inscriptions from the first millennium BCE that include mention of the Denyen.

However, it is essential to be careful about assessing destruction and whether it was the Sea People who were responsible. Initial findings can be refuted. A classic example is the archaeological site of Alaca Hoyuk. This was believed to be one of the preeminent acts of destruction at the end of the Hittite Empire. The first season of excavations in 1935 led to the conclusion that a violent assault leveled Alaca Hoyuk. This is not true. Excavations that followed indicated that there was no destruction around 1200 BCE that could be attributed to an invading force. The conclusion now is that the original findings were a scholarly invention and were not based on credible archaeological research (Millek, 2022).

Alaca Hoyuk is not the only site that is being viewed with skepticism. Some places that were once considered scenes of devastation by the Sea People were not that at all. For example, Miletus was once deemed to have been destroyed in 1200 BCE when, in fact, the damage was caused many years later. Likewise, Enkomi in Cyprus was labeled a place of Sea People destruction based on incomplete evidence from a limited excavation.

Regrettably, there are numerous instances where damage has been misstated based on scanty evidence or did not happen. The chance of false destruction is why earlier excavations must be re-examined. Earlier scholars may have been wedded to the idea of the Sea People destroying almost everything in the Late Bronze Age when it may have been earthquakes or other forces leveling the cities.

However, we cannot assume that the archaeologists at the time were deliberately duplicitous. The problem of false destructions may have been caused by the lack of a standard method of examining and defining arson and pillage. It may have simply been an issue of not having a set means of analyzing whether the ash deposits that were discovered were due to a city's sacking or only residue from industrial enterprises.

Egypt

The land of the pharaohs is a tremendous historical information center. This pre-modern civilization operating for three thousand years before the common era has provided us with copious amounts of information that allows scholars to dissect the history of an ancient world and civilization. The facts are strewn about everywhere.

The temples and tombs are primary sources of how the Egyptians lived. Entire walls are covered with inscriptions depicting daily life and significant events. The Egyptians could be very precise in their documentation. Researchers have learned from analyzing temple drawings of the droughts that affected Egypt and how such problems were solved by people who did not have computer technology.

The records of the reigns of the pharaohs report the interaction with numerous groups of people. What we have found in Egypt is a learning well of material on the Sea People. The Egyptians did not think of these pirates as merely a nuisance. On the contrary, the Egyptians felt they were a sizable threat to their country and explained how they dealt with the menace. The Egyptian records tell us perhaps the best accounts of who these water rovers were.

Secondary Sites

Egyptian pharaohs had stories of their military exploits carved into their tombs. These are one-sided accounts because the pharaohs did not mention their defeats. The engravings introduce us to various groups of the Sea People.

As indicated earlier, Ramesses II encountered the Sea People several times during his reign. He made a point of recording some of those experiences on the walls of his tomb and of temples he constructed and renovated.

The Tanis Stele II has an inscription that records an attack by the Sherden in the Nile Delta. In addition, the record on the stele mentions the problems that Egypt was starting to have with these waterborne outsiders:

"The unruly Sherden whom no one had ever known how to combat, they came boldly sailing in their warships from the midst of the sea, none being able to withstand them" (Wikipedia.org, 2023).

Another stele, the Aswan Stele, tells how Ramesses II defeated other Sea People in various battles.

Interestingly, although he fought against the Sea People, this pharaoh also employed Sea People in his military forces. As mentioned earlier, the captured Sherden were pressed into the ranks of the Egyptian army and fought at the battle of Kadesh. Ramesses had his scribes create an official description of the fight with copies sent to several places in Egypt, including Abydos, Karnak, Luxor, and Abu Simbel. One piece of royal information, the Poem of Pentaur, notes that the Sherden fought as allies against the Hittite Army (Wikipedia.org, 2023).

Temple at Karnak

Karnak was an ongoing construction project in which pharaohs made their own additions to the complex. It is one of the best sources of information about Egyptian history during this time. The Hall of Records is located in the north wing of the complex, and it contains scenes of the Sea People.

The Sea People are portrayed both as warriors and as prisoners. The reliefs show them as part of the spoils of war the Egyptians took. They are referred to as invaders from the sea and as vicious people who threatened the security of Egypt.

The Mortuary Temple of Ramesses II

Ramesses II was a prolific builder of temples and other buildings that recorded his greatness in addition to the history of Egypt in the 19th dynasty. The Mortuary Temple at Medinet Habu, a monument to this pharaoh, is practically a library of ancient Egypt's political and religious history. It is one of the best-preserved temples from the new kingdom. Moreover, it can be considered a depository of the record of Egypt and its conflict with the Sea People. The temple complex covers over 7,000 square meters and contains the main temple along with several smaller temples and administrative buildings. A massive mud brick wall over 10 meters high and 1.8 kilometers long surrounds the complex.

Ramesses III was a warrior king of the 20th dynasty. He spent most of his reign combating foreign threats to Egypt. The Sea People were a significant challenge to this pharaoh, who did not hesitate to confront them. He left inscriptions on the Mortuary Temple, which give a detailed explanation of the Sea People. The inscriptions are more than just factual accounts. Various observations that were not the inventions of royal propaganda can be found at Medinet Habu. Here we learn that Sea People were not a disorganized group of roving sea pirates. The idea that they were an alliance is on the temple's wall.

The scribes gave a name to them. The Sea People were referred to as the "Hau-nebut," which means "inhabitants of the Aegean." Interestingly, it appears that the Sea People played both sides of the field at the battle of Kadesh because the names of the individual tribes are noted as mercenaries who fought with the Hittites (Luwian Studies, 2023).

Ramesses III was no different than his predecessors when it came to boasting about his victories while ignoring any defeats:

"As for those who reached my boundary, their seed is not. Their hearts and their souls are finished unto all eternity. Those who came forward together upon the sea, the full flame was in front of them at the river mouths in the stockade of lances surrounded them on the shore" (Anderson, 2023).

Medinet Habu is the source of the widely-held opinion that the Aegean Sea was the starting point of the Sea People's activity and that considerable violence occurred in western and southern Anatolia.

A final inscription we would like to mention gives further insight into the Sea People and the havoc they wreaked on the Late Bronze Age:

"No land could stand before their arms, from Hatti, Qode, Carchemish, Arzawa, and Alasiya on, being cut off at one time. A camp was set up in one place in Amurru. They desolated its people and its land was like that which has never come into being. They were coming toward Egypt, the flame was prepared before them" (Kelly, 2021).

Egypt knew trouble was heading towards it.

Canaan

The records found in Canaan were not as extensive as those we have from Egypt and the Hittites. Still, the Canaanite information about the Sea People adds even more content to our understanding. The Hebrew Bible contains several references to the Sea People in its chapters.

The book of Judges describes the period when a series of judges ruled Israel and came under attack from the Sea People. The biblical references add weight to the prevailing opinion that the Sea People were a dangerous threat to the region's stability. The Hebrew Bible also hints that the descendants of the Sea People were in the area long after invasions ceased.

Sea People as a Trading Power

The Hebrew Bible tells us that the Sea People were not just pirates. The book of Ezekiel contains several references that mention the Sea People in regard to maritime commerce. Ezekiel 27:5-7 details activity between the Sea People and both Tyre and Egypt:

"They have made all by ship boards of first trees of Senir: they have taken cedars from Lebanon to make masts for thee. Of the oaks of Bashan have they made thine oars; the company of the Ashurites have made by benches of ivory, brought out of the aisles of Chittim. Fine linen with embroidered work from Egypt was that which thou spread us forth to be thy sail; blue and purple from the isles of Elisha was that which covered thee."

Ezekiel suggests that the Sea People were engaged in the trade of both sensible and luxury goods. If the Sea People were traders on the side, this poses a very interesting question.

Competition is always rough, and sea trade in the Late Bronze Age was no different. Ports were competing for business, and they would do what they could to eliminate their rivals. But were the Sea People engaged in getting rid of their competition? They naturally had booty on their mind when they entered a targeted seaport, but were they also intent on destroying the ships that lay at anchor? Such destruction would have been commercially advantageous.

Tel Dan

Those who read the Hebrew Bible might conclude that the Hebrews were one major nation of twelve tribes that emigrated from Egypt into Palestine. However, Tel Dan is an archaeological site in northern Israel that might contradict that assertion.

The Bible mentions that once Canaan was conquered by the Israelites, the tribes split the land among them. Dan was not included in the dispersal of property. Joshua 19:47 provides us with an account of what the tribe of Dan did:

"And the coast of the children of Dan went out too little for them: there for the children of Dan went up to fight against Leshem, and took it, and smote it with the edge of the sword, and possessed it, and dwelt therein, and called Leshem Dan after the name of their father" (Bohston, 2016).

The discoveries at Tel Dan point to a possible relationship between the Sea People and the tribe of Dan.

Assyria and Babylon

The evidence obtained from Syria and Babylon is less extensive than the material discovered in Egypt. Some inscriptions mention the Sea People, but nothing is in any significant detail. However, references as far away as the banks of the Euphrates and Tigris are examples of the Sea People's impact on the Late Bronze Age.

Carbon Dating

Modern technology permits us to go beyond inscriptions or reliefs on the walls of temples and tombs. Radiocarbon dating gives us some insight into Sea People's activity. This science allows researchers to better pinpoint when the Sea People were present in an area.

For example, radiocarbon results allow researchers to propose that the Sea People were in the northern Levant in 1194-1190 BCE. Combined with astronomical data, radiocarbon examinations showed us that the Sea People were attacking Ugarit sometime between 1192 and 1190 BCE.

Gibala is another site where radiocarbon dating tells of Sea People's presence. Gibala was an important trade center and was responsible for much of the wealth of the kingdom of Ugarit. Radiocarbon dating details the destruction of this settlement and hints about what happened in the area after the Sea People sailed away (David Kaniewski, 2011).

What is fascinating about the radiocarbon work done at Gibala is how closely it matches the historical dates that Egyptologists suggest for the reign of Pharaoh Mernetpath. The results also corroborate correspondence between Ugarit and the Hittite Empire. There was substantial trade activity in the area, and the radiocarbon dating notes that everything suddenly stopped.

The Sea People were a military force requiring substantial supplies of weapons to conduct their raids. These implements of war could not always be harvested from the battlefield. Arrows and spears needed to be mass produced, and it is doubtful the Sea People could secure ample supplies from their victims.

They needed to make their own, and it required certain materials. Bronze Age weapons were created using sophisticated metallurgical techniques, and certain elements were necessary. Two islands probably supplied the Sea People with what they needed to make military implements. The control of these may also have contributed to the damage done to the sea-borne commerce of the eastern Mediterranean.

Chapter 4 – Rape of Mycenae

The Mycenaean civilization was based in Greece and the islands of the Aegean Sea. It lasted from approximately 1400 to 1100 BCE. Its success was based on trade, and the Mycenaeans were expert seafarers and traders who used the water to their material advantage.

A form of feudalism was practiced in the region. A king was the head of the ruling class, with nobility and warriors making up the military. Peasants did the farming and produced wheat, barley, olives, and grapes. Trade goods included precious metals, luxury items, and raw materials.

The range of traffic included Greece and other areas of the Mediterranean Sea, including Egypt and Crete. The cities were commercial hubs, and they developed sophisticated markets and trading networks. The best-known cities were Mycenae, Tiryns, and Pylos.

This civilization had a sophisticated system of taxation and tribute, which helped generate wealth for the ruling elite. Tribute was usually paid in goods or services, and the taxes funded the construction of public works and monuments whose ruins are currently being investigated by teams of archaeologists. An example of the Mycenaean civilization's wealth includes the Treasury of Atreus, a tomb located near Mycenae. The tomb is made of massive stone blocks, and the interior features intricate carvings and decorations. Such tombs and other public works projects required tremendous amounts of labor and resources. These were available thanks to the prosperity that came with stable and predictable trade and commerce.

A political and social organization that favored the ruling elite helped ensure continued power and wealth. The aristocracy controlled the city-states' land and resources and oversaw the public works construction. They also maintained military and diplomatic alliances that were crucial factors in creating a stable power structure. Everything was there to create a social environment that was predictable and peaceful despite earthquakes and occasional local wars.

It appears that this civilization had what was required to flourish far into the future. But unfortunately, there were cracks in the surface that would eventually deepen and bring about a final collapse.

Military Ventures

Linear B tablets found in various archaeological sites give an idea of the military forces available to Mycenaean principalities. The evidence indicates that the military was not always small bands of men. Instead, Mycenaean kingdoms could recruit large groups of soldiers for combat duty. These troops were supplied with swords, spears, bows, and other implements of war. Bronze was the primary metal used to make these instruments.

The fortifications built to protect the cities were massive. They include high walls, gates, and towers. These were often made on elevated positions, and the outward appearance was one of almost impregnable military works. What seemed to be lacking was a sizable navy—the Mycenaean strength was in land forces and not sailors.

The Mycenaean civilization was busy, but it did not mean that it was peaceful. On the contrary, conflict constantly arose between the cities and states. We are not sure what all the reasons were for battle, but it is evident that diplomacy did not always work.

The Apparent Vulnerability

Conflict requires city armies to go on the offensive. The fighting between the Mycenaean states would mean that large numbers of men were absent from the city for extended periods. It is also possible that the aggression was carried out far from the home base. This means that the mother city or state was lightly defended at times and susceptible to surprise attacks.

The phrase "war means fighting and fight means killing" also includes "war is not cheap." Troops going off to war need to be paid and fed. The cash required to keep an army in the field would come from taxes and tributes levied on the common people. It's an onerous burden to carry, and heavy taxes are rarely appreciated.

The aggravation among the general population was exacerbated if the rulers could not adequately defend the homeland because the soldiers were far away fighting a war. The inability to protect fields and villages creates a social unrest that cannot be quickly quelled. Mycenaean kingdoms were very susceptible to rebellions caused by expensive wars. That vulnerability would get worse if, in the middle of a campaign, the state was suddenly hit by large bands of pirates operating in a hit-and-run fashion.

The Mycenaean tendency to go to war with each other created an opportunity the Sea People could exploit. Communication within the confederacy might have alerted commanders of the pirate fleets to the opportunities presented by war. The chances of success that resulted from insufficient troops to guard the walls or patrol the coast would be tempting. Unfortunately, the Sea People were not the kind of loot entrepreneurs to let an opportunity pass.

Significant Raids

Excavations have uncovered evidence that the Sea People attacked many places within the Mycenaean civilization. Here are several that stood out as targets for the sea pirates.

Pylos

Pylos was an influential Mycenaean city-state located on the southwest corner of the Peloponnesus. It is now a busy archaeological site, and the Palace of Nestor is a principal research dig. The Linear B tablets found in the Pylos archives give us considerable information about the Mycenaean culture and how it was administered. Pylos was an important trade center and controlled important trade routes that connected the eastern Mediterranean world.

Evidence from the excavations at the Palace of Nestor shows that the building was destroyed sometime in the later days of the 13th century BCE. The archives give a clue about what was happening at the time. There is mention of defense preparations being undertaken because of an attack that was coming. But unfortunately, the tablets give no detail about who was attacking and why it was happening.

Scholars believe that the Denyen were the Sea People who pillaged the city. The speculation is that the Denyen struck Pylos with an overwhelming force. The city's harbor was poorly defended, which added to the Sea People's advantage. The destruction of the city was total, and Pylos was not rebuilt.

The impact of the demise of Pylos was significant. Its loss seriously disrupted the maritime trade in the area and damaged the Mycenaean civilization's flow of goods and services. The region's economy was doubtlessly harmed, and there is no evidence that the area ever fully recovered from what was done.

Tiryns

This city-state was known as Tiryns of the high walls due to its significant fortifications. While earthquakes may have caused some of the damage to Tiryns, it does not explain the need to construct thicker walls. Instead, these defensive positions may have resulted from Sea People incursions, which damaged the city. Fortunately, Tiryns survived the period of the sea raids, although its status was significantly reduced.

Mycenae

Mycenae was the jewel in the crown. This was the cornerstone of the Mycenaean culture, and its influence stretched for miles beyond its municipal borders. Mycenae was in a naturally fortified position between Mount Sara and Profitis Ilias. Humans first occupied the location in the Neolithic age, and aristocracy was in place around 1700 BCE.

Mycenae was at the height of its power and glory at the start of the Late Bronze Age.

It was an important trading port, but it was also a manufacturing area. Weapons, tools, jewelry, carved gems, glass ornaments, and commonly used implements were created in the city's workshops.

Archaeological findings show that Mycenae was a well-fortified city whose walls were extended after an earthquake around 1200 BCE (Tornos News, 2018). It was a thriving city of great luxury with a highly organized feudal system. Its wealth and power, however, did not make it invincible. Mycenae was devastated in the Late Bronze Age and did not recover until the fifth century BCE.

Earlier theories of the city's downfall suggested that a series of earthquakes may have led to the destruction of Mycenae and its palaces. Those notions are no longer given much credence. Research conducted in the 21st century suggests another explanation.

German archaeologist Joseph Maran the Heidelberg University and his colleague geophysicist Klaus-G. Hinzen have studied the ruins since 2012. They reported significant findings in the *Bulletin of the*

Seismological Society of America:

"Although some of the observations from the two investigative settles could be explained by seismic loadings, alternative nonseismic causes could equally explain most observed damage. In some cases, the structural damage was clearly not caused by earthquakes... Our results indicate that the hypothesis of a destructive earthquake in Tiryns and Midea, which may have contributed to the end of the LBA Mycenaean palatial period, is unlikely" (Tornos News, 2018).

The old explanation needed to be replaced with a new one. Investigations conducted in the ruins indicated that areas were attacked and burned. The theory that the destruction was man-made is bolstered by large-scale strengthening and expansion of fortifications at various sites. Additionally, it appears subterranean passages were dug that led to underground cisterns. Finally, Mycenae itself doubled its fortified areas before its destruction.

The Peleset are believed to be the Sea People group that led the attack on Mycenae. Despite the burning and pillaging, the city eventually recovered from its plunder. But it never regained the significance it previously held.

The Analysis

Other Mycenaean cities that were targets of Sea People raids were Athens and Thebes. The attacks on Mycenaean cities are in addition to what probably happened on the high seas. Trading vessels were no doubt intercepted by the pirates, and this added to the economic disruption. In addition, well-established trade routes were damaged.

Scholars continue to search for conclusive evidence of what happened in Greece and the Mediterranean during the Late Bronze Age. However, it is safe to say that the Sea People did cause economic trouble.

Attacking a city and destroying large parts of it, if not the entire community, can result in a trade center being eliminated or knocked out of activity for an extended period of repair. Rebuilding a harbor can result in higher taxes. Crops burned during a pillaging raid harm the food supply, which may have already been stressed because of climate change. Any of these can put pressure on society and cause it to crumble.

An easy solution to the sea raids would be for the Mycenaean city-states to stop internal hostilities and declare a truce until the danger passed. Unfortunately, we do not have evidence this happened. Therefore, it is reasonable to assume that these local Greek states continued to battle with each other despite a more significant, comprehensive danger coming in just over the horizon. The unified opposition that could have prevented the chaos just was not there. Furthermore, there do not seem to have been any Mycenaean city-states with a naval force that could turn back the invaders. The entire civilization was a pigeon that was systematically plucked for years.

However, we do not think it is accurate or fair to accuse the Sea People of being the primary agent of the final collapse of the Mycenaean civilization. Indeed, the sea raiders probably added to an already troubling environment. There is enough evidence to suggest that things were going terribly wrong before the Sea People showed up.

The Mycenaean civilization was founded on a strictly hierarchical social system, which could lead to dissatisfaction among the lower classes. The raids proved that the ruling class was not able to protect anyone, which undoubtedly led to rebellion. Internal conflicts and social dissent, coupled with environmental difficulties and colossal migrations, may have weakened the Mycenaeans to such a degree that even large-scale pirate raids would not have been the only cause of a civilization's downfall. In short, Mycenaean culture was a rotted door that only needed to be kicked in to collapse. The Sea People may have provided that force.

Piracy in the Aegean Sea could have been stopped. Athens and Rome centuries later brought maritime brigandage to heel with fleets of ships assigned to destroy pirate bases. Unfortunately, it does not appear that the Mycenaeans could forget their internal differences long enough to create a strike force. Evidence suggests that at one point, a coalition did surface that turned the tables on the Sea People. However, Mycenae and its sister cities were too far gone to be resuscitated.

Social and economic opportunities helped the Sea People. Their activity probably caused a stream of refugees to move hither and beyond all of Greece. (Interestingly, some areas were not impacted by sea raids. Athens is an example of a city-state that appears to have successfully survived sea marauders.)

Greece went into a period known as the Dark Ages after the final destruction of the Mycenaeans, and it would not rebound until centuries later. As for the Sea People, the fall of the Mycenaean culture was not an insurmountable challenge to them. On the contrary, an even bigger prize awaited them to capture and successfully exploit.

Chapter 5 – The Hittite Collapse

Anatolia in modern-day Turkey was the home of the Hittites and the center of their empire. It included that region and extended to the western coast of Turkey and south into Syria. It was a significant presence in the Late Bronze Age, and its ruler was referred to as a Great King. The Hittites were able to conquer and dominate people in the region, and their military activity included campaigns against Egypt, resulting in one of the first recorded significant battles of history at Kadesh. All the kingdoms of the eastern Mediterranean recognized its military prominence, and its collapse after 1200 BCE came as a major shock.

Anatolian Majesty

The origins of the Hittites are still a bit of a mystery, but it seems they migrated from the Caucasus Mountains into Anatolia around 2000 BCE. Hittite society was rigidly hierarchical. At the top were the Great King and his family, who filled the highest offices of the state. Underneath them were the elite of the Hittite society who formed a hereditary nobility.

The aristocracy were owners of large estates that the kings conferred as fiefs based on the ability to provide military forces. In addition, the temples owned extensive tracts of land and were almost states within the state. Most Hittites were not part of the ruling class, but the local areas had their own regional upper class of landowners and merchants. What is noteworthy about the Hittite society is that it had many slaves, but these enslaved people had specific rights and could own property

(TimeMaps, 2023).

Imperial Administration

The Hittite Empire was comprised of a homeland surrounded by a cluster of smaller kingdoms that owed their allegiance to the Great King. As a result, a vassalage system emerged whereby a conquered enemy would give an oath of loyalty to the Great King and would then receive back his kingdom.

Vassals had considerable autonomy provided they gave tribute and provided required troops. The Hittite Great King committed to defending his vassals from external enemies and preserving the current ruling families. These vassals were not allowed to have any independent dealings with foreigners.

There was always the possibility of a vassal breaking away from the Hittites. Such rebellions were handled harshly. The primary city was sacked, and all inhabitants were carried off into serfdom. A new vassal ruler, ordinarily a Hittite prince, would be the replacement.

The Hittite Economy

The Hittites had a diverse economy built on several significant foundations. First, agriculture was a primary source of wealth. The homeland of Anatolia was not as productive as the river valleys of Egypt or the Fertile Crescent, but areas were producing a bountiful harvest. The Hittites used advanced irrigation techniques to cultivate wheat, barley, grapes, and olives. They also raised herds of livestock.

Second, metalworking was an essential source of wealth. The Hittites were skilled metallurgists and produced high-quality metal goods, notably weapons and tools, which were important trade items. Third, trade was essential. The Hittites had control of routes between the East and the West, enabling them to conduct business with neighboring states and distant civilizations, including some on the Silk Road. Trade items included metals, textiles, luxury goods, and agricultural products.

The Arts and Literacy

The empire erected palaces, temples, and fortresses that showed an advanced understanding of architecture. Its art was characterized by delicate design and pattern, particularly in metalwork. However, a more important part of the Hittite culture made them stand out. The Hittites were among the first to record laws, religious beliefs, and treaties. The cuneiform text they used allows us to take a deeper look into the governance of the empire, and the Hittites kept extensive records and correspondence.

The Hittite archives include numerous tablets written in Akkadian; a common language used in the Middle East at the time. Akkadian was the language of diplomacy. We have a better perception of the Hittite relations with their vassals and foreign kingdoms because of their use of a universal language. In addition, thousands of clay tablets provide a picture of Hittite society in the Bronze Age. The tablets also give clues about what finally brought down the empire (Beckman, 2023).

An Overwhelming Military Presence

The Hittites' ability to control an empire comprised of vassal states relied on their military prowess. The Hittites did not use bronze but rather iron weapons. This gave the Hittites a significant advantage on the battlefield and contributed to their military dominance in the region. However, weapons were only one reason for their success.

The Hittites could coordinate chariot attacks with their infantry, using the horse-drawn chariots to break enemy formations while their infantry attacked from the flanks. They were also experts at siege warfare and used advanced engineering techniques to breach city walls. The Hittites also maintained an advanced logistics system. They maintained a network of roads and bridges that allowed Hittite troops to move quickly to different parts of the empire. Fortresses and military outposts secured the borders and projected an image of overall military power.

All of this makes it appear that the Hittites were invincible and could repel any invader without much difficulty. That was the case for hundreds of years. The Late Bronze Age, however, introduced some stresses to the land of the Hittites that the ruling class could not adequately address, and the presence of the Sea People was a significant one.

The Vulnerability of the Empire

An apparent problem came from outside the borders. The Hittites had been able to fight the Egyptians to a standoff in the Levant, but there were significant enemies closer to home. The Assyrians based in northern Mesopotamia encroached on the Hittite territory in southeastern Anatolia. The Kassites were a demographic group from western Iran that created a kingdom in Babylon in the mid-16th century BCE and threatened Hittite sovereignty in the Levant.

The structure of the empire itself was a dilemma. The vassal states were different ethnic groups, and it became increasingly difficult to control them all. Rebellions kept springing up and had to be put down. The western part of the empire was a particularly contentious region. The Hittites had their hands full trying to maintain a sense of cohesion and were susceptible to unpredictable incursions. They were bound to protect their vassals from foreign invasions, and the inability to live up to that obligation was a sufficient reason for vassals to ignore Hittite suzerainty.

The economic power of the Hittites also rested on soft ground. Hittites relied heavily on trade and tribute to maintain the economy. Any disruption to commercial business would weaken the empire's economy. Moreover, the Hittites had to deal with outside competition, and any military action benefited their competitors.

Earlier, we mentioned the trouble that climate change caused in the region. Natural disasters such as earthquakes had damaged the economy, in addition to droughts. The Hittite Empire looked invincible from the outside. Unfortunately, once the façade is removed and a close investigation is conducted, the appearance is a magic show of smoke and mirrors. The Hittites were in trouble towards the end of the 12th century BCE and were about to face danger they were not adequately prepared to deal with.

The Hammer Blows

Historians pinpoint the zenith of the Hittite Empire as approximately the time of the battle of Kadesh with the Egyptians. The final collapse came only a few decades later. One interesting theory about the fall of the Hittites that includes elements of the Sea People involves the vassal states southwest of the Hittite homeland.

Cyprus is an island off the coast of Turkey that was noted for its copper resources in the Late Bronze Age. Control of the Cypriot mines was a compelling reason for the Hittite Great King, Tudhaliya, to attack Cyprus. (Another was the sea raids that originated there.)

Luwiya was an area comprised of several principalities in southwest Anatolia. The Luwians traded principally with Cyprus and relied on their commercial ties with that island. Therefore, the Hittite conquest of Cyprus was a serious disruption of trade that the Luwians did not appreciate.

Although they were vassals, the Luwians were not exceptionally loyal to the Hittites. They could quickly turn against the empire despite any obligations or commitments to the Great King. The petty kingdoms of Luwiya may have formed an alliance with other states, which was detrimental to the Hittites.

The theory postulates that the Luwians built a fleet of warships intending to overthrow Hittite control of the area. Their strategy was not to go overland to strike at Hattusa, the Hittite capital. Instead, this alliance of small states would weaken the empire by launching raids into Cyprus and Syria. If that was their intention, the Luwian coalition, now part of the Sea People, was very successful (Luwian Studies, 2023).

The Destruction of Ugarit

The clay tablets of the Hittite Empire provide a better picture of the Sea People's invasions than the Mycenaean records. Ugarit, a vassal city for the Hittites in northern Syria, would bear the brunt of an attack by the Sea People.

A primary source for what happened is the correspondence of a merchant of Ugarit, Urtenu, who documented trade and commerce in the region. Among the clay tablets he left behind were diplomatic letters. Urtenu was important enough to communicate with the rulers of Egypt, the Hittite Empire, Assyria, and Beirut, which he did on behalf of the king of Ugarit. He left behind a rather sobering account of what was happening in the region.

Correspondence from the Hittite Empire was dire. What started out as requests for help turned into desperate pleas as the region around Ugarit was hit by drought and famine. One desperate message from a local Hittite official gives an idea of the sense of desperation:

"If there is any goodness in your heart, then send even the remainders of the grain staples I requested and thus save me."

Bureaucrats were not the only people writing frantically to find a means of controlling hunger. Ammurapi, the king of Ugarit, sent an urgent request to the Egyptian pharaoh:

"In the land of Ugarit, there is a severe hunger. May my Lord save it. And may the king give grain to save my life...and to save the citizens of the land of Ugarit."

Famine was just the tip of the devastating iceberg. The king of Ugarit wrote in another correspondence of invaders showing up off the coast and creating a beachhead only five miles away from Ugarit. His letter was being sent to the viceroy of the Hittite vassal city-state of Carchemish:

"Send me forces and chariots and may my Lord save me from the forces of this enemy."

We do not know if the letter reached Carchemish. The excavations at Ugarit show evidence of hand-to-hand combat, and traces of fires that burned through the city have been discovered. However, nothing suggests that the city recovered from the attack (Atwood, 2021).

Alashiya

The kingdom of Alashiya is believed to have been located on Cyprus. It was a major copper producer and a place where the Hittites sent exiles. It was also a target of the Sea People, and there was correspondence from the king of Alashiya to the king of Ugarit requesting ships to help protect his country. This request for help is intriguing. One king of a vassal area requested assistance from another vassal of the Hittites; it was not sent directly to Hattusa. This raises the question of just how capable the Hittites were in defending their empire from maritime invasions. The Hittites were recognized as a formidable military force, but why could they not successfully counter the Sea People?

The Hittites Were Outmaneuvered

It often happens that the strongest point in a defense turns out to be the weakest link in the chain. The Hittites were victorious on land. Unfortunately, there is no clear evidence that the Hittites had a dedicated navy during the Late Bronze Age.

Ships were used for transportation and trade, and the Hittites did engage with the Sea People in several naval battles. Nevertheless, they had difficulty confronting highly mobile adversaries on the water. The essential battle tactics of the Sea People were mobility and unpredictability. As we know, hit-and-run raids were their specialty. Moreover, the naval technology advantage of the Sea People made it even harder to cope with the problems these pirates produced.

Coordinating a military response was difficult for the Hittites. They needed to call on the support of vassal states in addition to troops they raised from the homeland. It took time and effort to assemble a significant response to an emergency. Logistical planning and military organization were lacking. Sea People didn't have these coordination problems. They could strike hard and were long gone before any relief army appeared on the scene.

For these reasons, the Hittites were continually frustrated in their efforts to engage the Sea People. As a result, the empire could not adequately protect its coastal cities. This generated an even more significant problem. The vassal network created by the Hittites relied on the empire's ability to protect its client states. As it became increasingly clear that the Hittites could not do that, the response was not always the best when the empire called for military support from its vassals.

The vassal states had to look out for themselves. It caused them to question whether the relationship with the Hittite Empire was worthwhile. Moreover, the gradual weakening of the Hittites due to the raids allowed vassal states to advance their independence. Consequently, the Hittite Empire dealt with external danger and internal dissent.

The internal issues were not only centered on vassal-empire relationships. The ruling class was beginning to be seen as unable to govern and protect effectively. The Sea People's attacks only exacerbated challenges brought on by famine. The unrest and discontent were other nails being driven into the coffin.

The Fall of Hattusa

The Sea People incursions added to the problems that the Hittite Empire faced. Other forces were pressing in on and contesting for more territory. In 1190 BCE, a group of people known as the Kaskas sacked and burned Hattusa. The capital was eventually abandoned, and its devastation was a calamity the empire could not endure. It was the end of a state that once had premier authority for centuries.

Vassal states no longer saw the need to provide any tribute or support to an empire that had outlived its usefulness. The Hittite hegemony in the Middle East was now delegated to the dustbins of history, and modern archaeology would bring it back to widespread attention.

Once again, Sea People demonstrated how a sudden and devastating force could bring a thriving civilization to its knees. They exploited weaknesses that were becoming increasingly apparent and turned a series of successful raids into a driving force that ended the Mycenaean culture and the great empire of the Hittites.

As discussed, internal divisions were a significant part of the success of these raiders, as the Sea People's opponents could not bring together a unified force to meet the challenge they presented. However, this was going to change. The Sea People would soon face the resistance of unified nation-states.

Those countries had the resolve and resources the Hittites and the Mycenaeans could not call on. Moreover, the existence of a nation-state was a phenomenon the Sea People found extremely difficult to exploit.

Chapter 6 – The Copper Islands

We often think of plunder as gold, silver, and jewels. That is true, but those were not the only precious items worth stealing in antiquity. Pirates wanted to get their hands on other things with significant value.

Bronze is not an element like iron or gold. It is the product of several metals mixed together in a recipe to produce the material from which most weapons in the 13th and 12th centuries BCE were made. Control of copper determined the number of weapons a nation could use to defend itself. Whoever controlled the copper trade in the Late Bronze Age was in a kingmaker position. We suspect this was one of the objectives the Sea People were pursuing: several islands were rich sources of copper.

Sardinia was a primary source of copper in the 12th century BCE. There is evidence of numerous furnaces on the island that were used to make bronze implements and process copper so that the metal could be used for manufacturing elsewhere. The inhabitants of Sardinia were the Nuragic, and they could produce a variety of bronze objects, including daggers, swords, and axes (Wikipedia.org, 2023).

Sardinia was an essential weapons manufacturer throughout the Late Bronze Age. Moreover, it was an exporter of copper to metal-scarce areas such as the Mycenaean cities. The Sherden originated in Sardinia, and they would have had easy access to weapons since they were manufactured there.

Archaeometallurgy, which concerns itself with the production and past use of metals by ancient civilizations, lets us know more about copper's role in the Late Bronze Age. The researchers also examine the scale of production.

Foundries on Sardinia processed the raw copper that was coming from the mines. These were not the large-scale metal processors we ordinarily think of, and there were no blast furnaces the size of those used in the Industrial Age. The reason is quite simple: it was not necessary. The Industrial Revolution and modern society have a great demand for processed metal because of the use and the size of the population served. The needs of the Late Bronze Age were nowhere near as great. Still, copper was produced not only for ornament but for other uses.

Copper on Sardinia was made into ox hide ingots. They were metal slabs that resembled an ox hide and had protruding handles in each of the four quarters. Shaping copper into ingots made the metal easier to transport and meet the demand of societies that were dependent on bronze. This tells us that bulk copper was a desired commodity, and the recovery efforts of several shipwrecks suggest that ox-hide copper ingots could be a sizable portion of the ship's cargo (Schiavo, 2020).

There was more to Sardinia than just its ability to mine and refine copper so it could be used for making weapons. Bronze requires other components, and tin is essential. Tin was mined in Britain and Spain. The significance of Sardinia is that it was a logical stopping point for ships bearing tin to the eastern Mediterranean. The Sherden could easily purchase cargo from those ships, whose captains were only too willing to cut their voyage and risk short by unloading it in Sardinia.

The island provided the Sherden with the opportunity to make bronze. Additionally, they could control the amount of tin being shipped to prospective raiding targets. It would be difficult, if not impossible, for Mycenaean or Hittite manufacturers to get the metals they needed to process bronze weapons in large quantities if the deliveries were made in Sardinia. The Sherden literally had them by the throat and no doubt exploited the material advantage they possessed.

Crete

Another place the Sea People may have been looking for ox-hide copper ingots for later trade was Crete.

The island did have copper deposits (located in southern Crete), but the extent of the deposits indicates that Crete was not a significant producer of copper. However, Egyptian tomb paintings note that Crete was a primary source of ox-hide ingots and an exporter of copper. A sizable number of ingots were found near Kato Zakro. In addition, there is evidence that bronze was made during the earlier Minoan civilization, and bronze tools have been found that date to that time. The question is, where did Crete, which did not have substantial deposits of copper, get the elemental metal for bronze production? (Tamara Stech Wheeler, 2023)

A probable source of the copper was Cyprus. This island had vast deposits of the metal, and trade between Crete and Cyprus would include ox-hide ingots being traded for ceramics and other commodities. Crete's familiarity with bronze manufacturing made it an ideal place to make bronze implements. There were already well-established trade relations between Egypt and Crete, making Egypt a primary training partner. Mycenaean city-states might also be places where Crete shipped both ingots and implements. There is also evidence of trade between Crete and cities in the Levant. Crete was a major player in the sea economy of the eastern Mediterranean during the days of the Minoan culture, and it continued to be important in the Late Bronze Age. Crete can be considered a floating distribution center south of the Aegean Sea.

Evidence suggests that the Peleset originated in Crete. A primary source is the Phaistos Disk. This artifact has been cited as proof that the Philistines, believed to be the Peleset, originated in Crete. The Hebrew Bible adds further weight to this association by stating in Jeremiah 47:4 that Capthor is where the Philistines originally came from. Therefore, Capthor could have been Crete. The Tjekker might also have viewed Crete as their homeland (Associates for Biblical Research, 2006).

The relationship between Crete and the Sea People includes some cultural similarities. The Cretans had similar pottery and metalwork, along with a mutual preference for certain kinds of jewelry. It is possible there were strong trade relations between the two groups, and there is little to suggest that Crete was assaulted the way other places in the eastern Mediterranean were.

Copper goods and ox-hide ingots were exported from Crete all over the eastern Mediterranean. It suggests that the Sea People were influential in distributing a strategically important metal during the Late Bronze Age. That dominance made the Sea People more than just a band of raiders. They were influencers who could disrupt trade and determine where copper was going and what places would be denied ready access to this valuable strategic resource.

Cyprus

The relationship between Cyprus and copper is best shown by the fact that the word copper is derived from the Greek name for the island, *Kupros*. Tombs uncovered from the Late Bronze Age show the quality and quantity of metal products from Cyprus. There was significant demand for Cypriot copper, and evidence of goods created on the island stretches to the Black Sea and Babylonia. The impact of copper production on the Cypriot culture was significant. Economic power and trade were tied to the production of the ingots, and the ruling elite kept strict control of it.

Significant copper-bearing ore deposits were discovered on the north slope of the Troodos Mountains, and Cypriot sites such as Ambelikou-Aletri were mining centers. The tin necessary for creating bronze had to be imported, but Cyprus had all the copper it needed to become a major bronze center in the Late Bronze Age. An example of how much copper was mined in Cyprus is the Ulu Burun shipwreck. Discovered off Turkey's southwestern coast, the cargo had over ten tons of Cypriot copper (Hemingway, 2004).

The village of Hala Sultan Tekke furnishes a significant example of just how sophisticated Cypriot production of copper was during the Late Bronze Age. The town was located near the mines of the Troodos Mountains, close to the modern-day city of Larnaca. In addition, Hala Sultan Tekke had a well-protected harbor, and evidence indicates a considerable amount of trade activity in this larger-than-ordinary village (University of Gothenburg, 2023). Excavations indicate extensive copper production. Cast molds, smelting furnaces, and slack were found at the site. Apparently, these workshops involved with copper production were placed in the north of the city so that soot could be blown away by the winds that came from the south.

Other places in Cyprus were connected closely with copper and trade, including Kitipn, Enkomi, and Maroni.

The kingdom of Alashiya on Cyprus was a significant player in the economic world of the Late Bronze Age. Cuneiform letters were sent from Alashiya to the Egyptian pharaoh, and there were high-level diplomatic trade relations between Cyprus and the Middle East. The copper trade was highly organized, and there is evidence of state agents conducting foreign business. Product diversity and shipping capacity were everyday matters. Cyprus had the attention of everybody in the eastern Mediterranean, which was not always a good thing.

Cyprus and the Hittites

The Great King of the Hittite Empire had his eye on Cyprus. Essential grain shipments were being disrupted by pirates using Cyprus as a base for attacks on shipping; consequently, the Hittites tried to take control of the island in a series of military engagements. Great King Suppiluliuma II defeated the Alashiyans in the first recorded sea battle in history. He also launched a land attack.

The consequence of the aggression was that the Hittite Empire subjugated Cyprus. It was a significant victory but turned out to be a Pyrrhic one.

The ships and men used to take over Cyprus were not available to protect the coast from any raids. This meant that understaffed garrisons had to face invasions of Sea People, and many were left vulnerable because the best men were off fighting somewhere else. Stripping the coast of needed soldiers perhaps caused that frantic letter from the ruler of the vassal kingdom of Ugarit begging for help—but receiving no reply.

Cyprus and the Sea People

Cyprus was valuable for usable deposits of copper, but there were other reasons for the Sea People to be interested in the island. It was strategically located near the sea lanes of the Aegean Sea and the eastern Mediterranean, so pirate ships could easily intercept trade vessels and take valuable cargo. Furthermore, it was a good base for operations.

Sea People ships could lay at anchor along the coast, resupply, and take the opportunity to rest their crews and plan other operations. There was no need to try to control the entire island. The ability to influence copper production and trade and use Cyprus as a naval base were sufficient reasons to exploit it.

There are scholarly discussions about whether Cyprus was a great gathering place from which the Sea People launched a coordinated attack on Egypt. There is no current evidence to suggest this happened. Nevertheless, this does not mean the island was not employed as a staging point for large-scale raids along the coast of Anatolia.

The Sea People were doing more than just wreaking havoc on the Anatolian coast. Their activity in the copper islands indicates they gradually gained control over most of the copper production in the eastern Mediterranean. Copper was an essential metal that everyone depended on. Therefore, the Sea People played a significant role in producing and distributing a highly strategic metal.

This raises some interesting possibilities. The Sea People could influence the amount of copper exported to various states. They could reduce the supply if they wanted to, or if they chose, they could manipulate the price of the commodity. Either way, it was in the Sea People's power to weaken a nation's ability to respond effectively to attacks. The lack of copper weapons or the rising cost of copper could inflict a severe economic strain on places already experiencing problems with famine or internal dissent.

We must have corroborating evidence to determine if the Sea People deliberately weakened their targets before a raid. However, they could if they chose to do it. If so, weakening their prospective victims through economic pressure makes them look more formidable.

Everything that the Sea People were doing fit into an excellent plan for success. They dominated the sea trade routes, heavily influenced the export of copper, and had a perfect strategy for dealing with targeted areas. However, a few decades later, they realized they were nowhere near as powerful as they thought. A black swan would be floating into their waters.

Chapter 7 – The Treasure Chest Called Egypt

The most extensive records we have of the Sea People come from Egypt. While the Hittites did have clay tablet archives, their data collection on the Sea People is not as impressive as what was discovered in Egypt. We have detailed explanations in the hieroglyphics and a better idea of what the Sea People looked like from the reliefs carved into the tombs and temples.

An Embarrassment of Riches

Egypt was the wealthiest nation of the Late Bronze Age. Its wealth derives from Egypt possessing impressive qualities that fostered abundance.

- Geography

Egypt was situated at the crossroads of trade routes connecting Asia, Europe, and Africa. Its strategic position allowed Egypt to control the flow of goods and ideas between these continents, giving it a significant advantage in commercial terms. Additionally, the Nile River, which flowed through Egypt, provided the country with fertile land for agriculture.

- Control of the Trade Routes

Egypt was in control of the land and sea routes that connected the Mediterranean and the Red Sea, making the country a crucial hub for trade between the three continents. Egyptians were expert sailors and traders. They established a sophisticated trading network that extended far beyond the borders of their country. Egyptian merchants prospered in the luxury goods trade, including gold, ivory, spices, and precious stones.

- Agricultural Abundance

Farming was a vital source of wealth. Egypt's fertile land, irrigated by the Nile, allowed the Egyptians to grow crops such as wheat, barley, and flax, which were essential for economic prosperity. Egyptians were also skilled in animal husbandry, and they raised cattle, sheep, and goats for meat, milk, and wool. Additionally, Egypt was rich in natural resources such as copper, gold, and precious stones.

Wealth made Egypt powerful and vulnerable at the same time. Egypt was a superpower whose diplomats were welcome guests at the palaces of rulers throughout the region. However, this mighty nation was vulnerable to foreign invasion. Egypt, through the centuries, was attacked by outside forces wishing to take the wealth Egyptians produced. The Sea People were among the more significant challenges faced by the land of the pharaohs. Egypt was a prize that the Sea People wanted for themselves.

Ramesses II

Ramesses II, also known as Ramesses the Great, ruled Egypt from 1279 BCE to 1213 BCE. We know from the records carved on the temples he built that Ramesses had contact with the Sea People during his reign.

His most significant exposure to the Sea People was in one of his best-known military campaigns.

Egypt had complex relations with Hittite Empire, and one dispute led to a campaign that culminated in the battle of Kadesh. This is considered one of the most significant chariot battles in history. Ramesses made a point of having the battle recorded and inscribed on the temple walls of Abu Simbel.

Among the warriors depicted was a group of Sea People, the Sherden. The wall carvings display the Sherden as prisoners taken by the Egyptians. It is one of the first times we have a pictorial record of Sea People. Interestingly, the same inscriptions describing the battle also portray other Sea People fighting for the Egyptians as mercenaries (Mark, 2009).

Kadesh was not the first time Ramesses had encountered the Sea People. Earlier, he fought a naval battle with the Sherden and decisively defeated them. The accounts that Ramesses left imply he had removed the Sea People as a threat to Egypt because of his military prowess. History proves he was incorrect.

Merneptah

Ramesses II lived to an advanced age and outlived most of his children. His reign was more than sixty years, and the succession following his death created some political instability. His successor, Merneptah, was his fifteenth son and was an old man when he finally became pharaoh. Therefore, it was an opportunity for outside forces to try their luck in overthrowing the established order. Fortunately for Egypt, Merneptah was carefully groomed to be pharaoh and was ready for the challenges he was facing. Merneptah ruled for ten years and was forced to spend his golden years fighting off serious invasions. He used several means to deal with the Sea People.

- Military Measures

Merneptah was confronted with an alliance of the Libyans and the Sea People. He waged an aggressive military campaign against both and scored a significant victory in battle. The triumph and other successful campaigns prompted the pharaoh to have accounts of his achievements inscribed in various places. One of the commemorative texts can be found on the sixth pylon at Karnak and includes a listing of enemies Merneptah fought and defeated. The inscription has the following to say about the Sea People:

"The wretched, fallen chief of Libya, Merye, son of Ded, as fallen by the country of Tehenu with his bowmen—Sherden, Shekelesh, Ekwesh, Lukka, Teresh. Taking the best of every warrior and every man of war of his country. He has brought his wife and children-leaders of the camp, and he has reached the western boundary in the fields of Perire."

We need to remember that commemorative inscriptions and stela commissioned by the pharaohs were always full of bombastic praise given to the monarch. Despite possible overstatement, it is clear that the old pharaoh successfully addressed a threat to Egypt (Wikipedia.org, 2023).

- Diplomacy

Merneptah led an army that was well-trained and well-equipped. However, it would take more than the force of arms to deal with a confederacy such as the Sea People. The pharaoh recognized this and used a divide-and-conquer strategy that employed diplomatic relations and alliances.

Merneptah made a treaty with the Libyans that established peaceful relations between the two parties and allowed for the free movement of trade and people across the borders. It also allowed Egypt to use its military force against the Sea People. Merneptah even established diplomatic relations with some of the Sea People tribes and created alliances that could put more military pressure on the sea raiders.

- Economic Efforts

Merneptah understood that the Sea People were motivated by the desire for plunder and would lose interest in attacking Egypt if there were fewer opportunities to pillage and steal. Accordingly, he took measures that would decrease any chance of profitable attacks. A system of forts and garrisons was created to protect Egypt's borders from the pirates, and these defenses were also intended to control the movement of goods and people along Egypt's northern coastline. Merchants, traders, and other travelers were required to stop in the forts and obtain permits to proceed. In addition, a system of checkpoints created by these forts allowed the Egyptians to monitor the movement of people and goods. It made it harder for the Sea People to enter Egypt undetected.

Merneptah also worked on the maritime infrastructure of the Egyptians. Building harbors, docks, and other naval facilities allowed Egypt to control its coastal waters better and reduce the possibility of surprise attacks. As a result, Egypt was better able to manage its maritime trade.

Furthermore, he created a trade and commerce network that persuaded other regional powers to ally with Egypt. It made it difficult for the Sea People to gather additional support from possible partners. Of course, the Sea People could profit from all of this. Merneptah's efforts allowed the Sea People to engage in legitimate trade and commerce with Egypt, particularly those tribes with diplomatic relations.

The aging monarch addressed the problem of the Sea People with proactive measures and successfully defended Egypt from the outset attacks. This, unfortunately, proved to be a short-term success. The Sea People were not finished with their attempts to ravage Egypt.

Ramesses III

The 19th, or Ramesside, Dynasty of Egypt ended in 1189 BCE. The Twentieth Dynasty, which lasted from 1189 to 1077 BCE, was the last one of the New Kingdom Period, and historians regard the Twentieth Dynasty as the beginning of the decline of Ancient Egypt. The most notable pharaoh of this period was Ramesses III, who reigned from 1186 to 1155 BCE.

The new pharaoh ascended the throne after a period of political unrest in Egypt. Internal troubles always created opportunities for foreign nations, and Ramesses III was forced to protect Egypt from external assault. He first had to deal with a coalition of Libyan tribes and defeated them in the Western Nile Delta. It did not bring on a period of prolonged peace because the next threat to his throne came from an even larger and more dangerous adversary: the Sea People. And it was more than just a raid on the Delta.

The attack was more a migration of displaced people than a looting expedition. The Sea People had more on their minds than stealing gold and jewels from Egypt. Instead, they wanted permanent placement in the land of the pharaohs, and they were not going to ask for some property. Instead, they intended to take what they wanted.

Djahy

Ramesses III was required to meet the Sea People in multiple engagements. The initial one occurred in 1178 BCE at Egypt's eastern frontier in what is now Lebanon. It was a land battle at a place called Djahy.

The Sea People had attacked Kadesh and decided that they would try their luck in attacking Egypt. Inscriptions found at Medinet Habu provide the background for the battle itself:

"The foreign countries conspired in their islands. All at once the lands were removed and scattered in the fray. No land could resist their arms. From Hatti, Kode, Carchemish, Arzawa and Alashiya on-being cut off at one time. A camp was set up in Amurru. They desolated its people, and its land was like that which had never existed. They were coming forward towards Egypt, while the flame was prepared for them. Their Confederation was the Peleset, Tjekker, Shekelesh, Denen, and Weshesh, lands United. They laid their hands upon the lands as far as the circuit of the earth, their hearts were confident and trusting as they said 'our plans will succeed!'"

This text from the temple tells us that the Sea People were now moving across land and had a high degree of success against other countries. The number of Sea People groups in the invasion force gives an idea of the enormity of what was facing the Land of the Pharaohs. It was an assault the Egyptians had not met since the invasion of the Hyksos and, if successful, would have destroyed Egypt the way the Mycenaeans and the Hittites fell.

Fortunately for Egypt, Ramesses III was able to bring his army out into the Levant. The battle that finally happened was a great victory for the Egyptians, and Ramesses commemorated the outcome:

"The Egyptian chariots are warriors... and all good officers. Their horses are ready to crush strangers under their hooves... Those who reach my border, out of their seat are not, their hearts and souls are dead forever and ever."

To put it plainly, Ramesses inflicted a decisive defeat on the land-born Sea People force. It was his triumph, but he could not rest on his laurels. There was an even more significant threat from the Sea People to his country, and it would strike at the heartland of Egypt (Cleopatra Egypt Tours, 2023).

The Sea People were stung at Djahy because they did not have the opportunity to use their navy to good advantage. However, it did not deter them because they still had a superior fleet. And, if their attack by land was unsuccessful, perhaps their assault by sea would be more so.

Battle of the Delta

The Egyptians were no match for the Sea People in open water. Their sailors were not as skilled, and the ships of the Sea People were technically superior. So, realizing the odds were against him in a sea battle, Ramesses laid a trap. He permitted the fleet of the Sea People to sail into the Nile Delta without opposition. In doing so, Ramesses had the perfect battleground. His ships were more maneuverable within the Delta, which gave the Egyptians an advantage. He placed archers on the banks of the Nile to prevent his enemy from landing, and he also had bowmen on the decks of the Egyptian ships. The Sea People were only armed with swords and spears. The enemy was thus not able to counterattack effectively. The Egyptians gained a further advantage by using grappling hooks to capsize enemy ships (Ancient-origins.net, 2015).

The Battle of the Delta was a definitive victory for the Egyptians. They successfully defeated a significant attempt to conquer the land. Ramesses III deserved credit for the success. The pharaoh recorded his triumph at the temple of Medinet Habu:

"As for those who had assembled before them on the sea, the full flame was their front before the harbor mouths, and a wall of metal upon the shore surrounded them. They were dragged, overturned, and laid low upon the beach; slain and made heaps from stem to bow of their galleys while all other things were cast upon the water" (Wikipedia.org, 2023).

The pharaoh's bragging did not consider the toll the Sea People's attacks inflicted on his nation. His army was exhausted from all the fighting, and the treasury was drained. Egypt won the battle, but winning peace would be a different story. Egypt was so severely damaged by the experience that it could not fully recover from the shock. Egypt's glory days were over, and it began a slow decline that lasted centuries (Vuckovic, 2020).

Historian Marc van de Miroop notices something interesting about the Egyptian records of the Sea People: Merneptah and Ramesses III depict the Sea People's invasions as unexpected. That is a curious assessment, given the amount of activity in the Aegean Sea and against the Hittite Empire. This suggests the Egyptians may have considered them friends at one point.

The confusion is the result of a strategic mistake made by the pharaohs. The Egyptians hired the Sea People as mercenaries—a short-term decision that would have long-term consequences. The Romans also hired foreigners as auxiliaries. One of them, Arminius, a cavalry officer, led Germanic tribes in the massacre of several Roman legions in the Teutoburg Forest. Mercenaries can examine their employers' inner workings, and that can be dangerous.

In this case, it allowed these foreigners to examine the military structure of the Egyptian army, its battle tactics, and strategic priorities. Furthermore, these strangers also had the chance to explore the social network of Egypt and its foreign policy. They had an opportunity to find out who the Egyptians thought were enemies and who were friends. All of this is internal intelligence that can be used against higher mercenaries. It would not be surprising if the Sea People took their intimate knowledge of the Egyptian government and military and used it against Egypt.

Egypt Survived

The Mycenaean culture and Hittite Empire collapsed in the face of the onslaught of the Sea People. Egypt survived the assault. We have some ideas about how Egypt succeeded where other significant powers in the Late Bronze Age failed.

- Egypt had a history

Egyptian civilization was ancient at the time of the Sea People incursion. That history was not simply carved on temple walls; it was written down on papyrus scrolls. Papyrus could survive for centuries, and records that were hundreds of years old were available to the pharaoh. Those accounts were probably not for public consumption. They would have documented challenges and setbacks that earlier rulers encountered and how they dealt with them. Egypt had been invaded before, and the Hyksos were a more significant threat to the Egyptian civilization than the Sea People ever were. Yet, Egypt was able to overthrow these foreigners. The hidden records would show how earlier problems were dealt with and what strategies to use. These tales from the past would be valuable when present and future foreign attacks occurred.

- Egypt was an actual nation-state

The Hittite Empire was a core homeland surrounded by vassal states. Any one of those vassals might rebel against the empire or attempt to secede. Egypt was a nation-state and not merely a collection of tribes.

The relationship between the pharaoh and the Egyptian people was firm and could not be denied. Pharaoh was a living God and not just a monarch. The Egyptian people held a degree of reverence for their ruler that had been reinforced by years of continuity.

Pharaoh was not just someone who enjoyed the pleasures of being in control. Egyptian history makes clear that the pharaohs had a sense of responsibility to the people that made these monarchs feel a commitment to their common welfare. An attack on Egypt meant there would be a firm response, and the pharaoh would lead it. Whether they were peasants, traders, priests, or even slaves, those who lived in Egypt knew that when danger arose, the attention of their king was riveted on ending the emergency as quickly as possible.

- There was a dependable fourth estate

Pharaoh had a strong relationship with the priest caste of Egypt. Those attendants of the temples had granaries connected to the places of worship so that in times of famine or war, there was a ready source of food to be rationed. The priests also kept the records, including all of the commemorative statues and stela. They could communicate the commitment of the pharaoh to the population in any emergency. Their influence could not be underestimated. The morale of citizens is essential in times of war, and the priests could be used to keep everyone's spirits up.

The Sea People vanish from the Egyptian record after the Battle of the Delta. Egypt was hit hard by the Sea People, but it survived, and that is the most critical consideration. Other nations in the eastern Mediterranean had difficulty dealing with these seafaring raiders and collapsed before the onslaught of the Sea People. But one other place met the sea raids with a firm resolution and commitment to turning back the Sea People.

Chapter 8 – The Land of Milk, Honey, and Invasion

Canaan was an ancient region on the eastern Mediterranean coast that encompassed parts of modern-day Israel, Lebanon, Palestine, and Syria. It cannot be considered a major power in the region, such as Egypt or the Hittite Empire, but it had considerable significance, nevertheless.

Canaan was located at the crossroads of several trade routes and had access to both the Mediterranean Sea and the Jordan River. It was an important center of trade and commerce, and its cities and ports served as vital hubs for the flow of goods and people between the eastern Mediterranean and other parts of the world. Canaan was located on a natural land bridge between Asia and Africa, allowing it to influence commerce and migration between the two continents. It was a territory that would spark the interest of any bandits, and the Sea People knew its strategic and commercial value.

The Sea People in Canaan

The Sea People's understanding of Canaan may have been intimate. Egyptian records suggest that Ramesses III may have settled the Sea People in Canaan to serve as a buffer group between Egypt and the Hittite Empire. Scholars debate this, and there is no consensus on whether the Pharaoh indeed authorized a forced settlement. Nevertheless, Ramesses III states in the Harris Papyrus that he settled Sea People in various areas:

"I settled them in stronghold, bound in my name. Numerous were their classes like hundred-thousands. I tax them all, and clothing and grain from the storehouses and granaries each year" (Biblical Historial Context, 2023).

The Sea People included family in their attack on Egypt, however. It is also possible that those Sea People who were not killed or captured returned to the area of Canaan and settled. Either way, there is a likely chance they shared information with their seaborne relatives (Lacey, 2022).

Wealth might not have been the only reason for attacking Canaan. There was a confederation, but that did not mean there was a unity of purpose. Each ethnicity within the confederacy had its own goals and objectives, and some of the Sea People were either allies or mercenaries of the Hittite Empire and Egypt. Canaan may have been viewed as a place for settlement by some of the Sea People.

A final reason for taking Canaan is that the opportunities presented by the Mycenaean culture and the Hittite Empire were dwindling, and Egypt was too strong to be subjugated. Canaan was still a viable territory for plunder.

A city that was closely connected to the Sea People was Tyre, also known as Teresh. A passage from Ezekiel contains a prophecy that includes a subtle reference to the Sea People:

"This is what the Lord God says to Tyre: Will not the coastlines quake at the sound of your downfall, and the wounded grown at the slaughter in your midst? **All the princes of the sea will descend from their thrones, remove their robes, and strip off their embroidered garments. Clothes with terror, they will sit on the ground, trembling every moment, appalled over you.** Then they will lament for you saying, how you have perished, **O city of the renown inhabited by seafaring men-she who was powerful on the sea along with her people, who imposed terror on all peoples.** Now the coastlines tremble on the day of your downfall; the **islands in the sea are dismayed by your demise**" (Futile World, 2021).

Canaanite Targets

Ugarit was a sea state bordering on Canaan, and the Sea People devastated it as their raiding parties were destroying the Hittite Empire. There were other places, however, that were attacked from the sea.

- Ashkelon

   Ashkelon was a major city on the southern coast of modern-day Israel. Ashkelon was a trade center known for extensive maritime trade networks.

- Ashdod

   Ashdod was another major city on the southern coast. It was rebuilt after its attack but would not regain its former status as a major center of trade and commerce.

- Jaffa

   Jaffa is located in the area of modern-day Tel Aviv. It was a major Egyptian supply depot, and rail granaries were maintained there. The city may have been the victim of the Sea People's invasion of Egyptian border territory during the reign of Merneptah. Excavations have indicated that Jaffa was destroyed during a military campaign (Ancient Near East, 2023).

Other Canaanite cities that were attacked included Gaza, Sidon, and Lachish.

Obstacles to the Sea People

The Sea People had a fairly easy time of it when attacking Greek cities and the fringes of the Hittite Empire. Canaan was a different story. Bringing this area to its knees would not be a simple campaign.

Canaan had a history of being a battleground. The Hittites and the Egyptians fought over various areas of the region, and there were Egyptian fortresses and strong points. Canaanite cities were accustomed to being besieged and surviving the experience. They had the defensive positions required to hold off invading armies for long periods. That was not in line with the hit-and-run tactics of the Sea People.

The area also had a strong maritime history. Unlike the Hittites, Canaanite cities had naval expertise and could defend themselves against seaborne attacks. They could fight off incursions and conduct maritime trade at the same time. Canaan had geographical advantages. The Carmel range was a natural defense, and so was the Jordan River. If necessary, Canaanite forces could retreat to those locations and then come back at an opportune time. While not as formidable as the Egyptians, the Canaanite people had resources that would allow them to absorb a seaborne assault and survive.

Two groups of Canaanite people did not hesitate to confront the raiders.

The Phoenician Foe

The first encounter between the Phoenicians and the Sea People occurred when the Phoenician city of Sidon was attacked. Sidon was sacked and burned, but it was not abandoned. The Phoenicians rebuilt Sidon and worked on their naval defenses.

The Phoenicians were similar to the Sea People when it came to maritime expertise. Phoenicians were known for their skill in shipbuilding and navigation, and they could build fast and maneuverable ships. This meant they could take the fight to the Sea People on the open water. Phoenicians responded with the larger and more heavily armed ships. In addition, they developed effective coastal defenses. A system of coastal watchtowers allowed them to monitor the movements of the Sea People and thus respond quickly to any attacks.

The Phoenicians did more than build great ships and watchtowers. They allied with other coastal city-states and kingdoms, permitting them to pool resources and coordinate defenses. The Phoenicians also used subterfuge to confuse and mislead the Sea People. They would set false signals and light fires in different locations, making it difficult for the Sea People to identify the positions of Phoenician fleets. The Phoenicians were mindful of what the Sea People could do, but they were not afraid of their enemy. The lack of fear and confidence in what they could do to respond were significant reasons the Phoenicians did not crumble before the attacks.

The Hebrews

The Phoenicians were not the only formidable adversaries the Sea People encountered. Another group was an association of tribes bound together by customs and religion. This group would take the field against any incursion from the sea. These were the Hebrews.

According to the Bible, the Hebrews were a group of Semitic-speaking tribes that migrated from Egypt at about the same time the Sea People were raiding coastlines. They were basically a pastoral and agricultural society. They were not yet a centralized monarchy, and kinship ties and clan loyalties were the basis of their political and social organization.

One Religion United All

The Hebrew tribes were descendants of the sons of a man named Jacob, who was later renamed Israel. Each tribe had its own territory, and they were loosely confederated under the leadership of judges. Those judges were not monarchs but military and religious leaders responsible for maintaining order and defending the tribes against external threats.

What made these people unique was their monotheistic religion. They worshiped one god, Yahweh, and this one religion united the tribes.

The Hebrews' background as shepherds and farmers did not mean they were a passive lot at all. The book of Exodus in the Bible tells of how this tribal assembly fought its way out of Egypt and into Canaan. They had stood up against various Canaanite tribes and successfully defeated them. The Hebrews could defeat larger and better-equipped enemy armies because they were experts at war who used ambushes and hit-and-run tactics. Moreover, they made use of natural fortifications such as hills and mountains. The Hebrews would bend but not break.

The Hebrews did not have a standing army during the Sea People raids. They relied on tribal levies to defend their land, and each tribe was responsible for providing a certain number of fighting men who would be mobilized whenever needed.

The Philistines and Judges

One theory suggests that the Sea People did not stay on the coastline but could have settled as far inland as the Transjordan. This observation is based on findings at the Tell Abu al-Kharaz digs, which provided evidence of pottery and loom weights that matched the contemporary material culture of places where the Sea People came from (Zion, 2014).

Other evidence indicates that the Sea People were the Philistines mentioned in the Bible. It is argued that a severe famine in Anatolia was the primary reason for the Sea People to invade Canaan.

A major source of Hebrew information about the Sea People comes from the book of Judges in the Bible. This part of the Old Testament describes the period of history from the death of Joshua to the rise of the Israelite monarchy. During this time, the Israelites were ruled by a series of judges supposedly chosen by Yahweh to deliver the Hebrews from enemies.

The first encounter with the Philistines occurred during the time of Sampson, who was a judge famous for his incredible strength. Sampson was from the tribe of Dan, and according to the book of Judges, he was called upon by Yahweh to deliver the Hebrews from Philistine oppression.

We should read the accounts of Sampson and his fights against the Philistines with skepticism. However, the stories illustrate the Hebrews' resistance against the Philistines.

Gleaning information from the book of Judges allows us to better understand the impact the Philistines had on the Hebrews and the struggle between these two. In addition to the story of Samson, other passages mention the conflict.

Judges 3:31 describes an incident in which an Israelite judge named Shamgar killed six hundred Philistines, and this is an indication of the presence of the Philistines in the region and the hostility they showed towards the Hebrews.

Judges 10:6-9 describes a period of history after the death of Jair, during which time the Hebrews strayed from the worship of Yahweh and served the gods of the region. Because of this, Yahweh allowed the Philistines to oppress the Israelites for several years.

Judges 14-15 is about a contemporary of Sampson named Jephthah. Jephthah was a judge called upon to defend the Hebrews against the Philistines, who had taken control of several Hebrew cities. The account includes several battles with the Philistines, including how Jephthah killed thirty Philistines.

The Tribe of Dan

Judges 5:17-18 contains the song of Deborah, which is an account of a victory over a Canaanite king, Jabin. Speculation has it that the Sea People were part of the coalition Jabin assembled. As shared earlier, this passage of the book of Judges contains an interesting line:

"And Dan, why he abide with the ships?"

The Hebrews were primarily farmers and shepherds, but it looks as though the tribe of Dan did not fit that description. This line from the Bible is curious and may shed light on them.

To expand on this idea, we must consider that when the Hebrews left Egypt, they were not the full twelve tribes the Bible would have us believe. The tribe of Dan was left out in the distribution of land among the Hebrew tribes. This oversight might have been intentional if the tribe of Dan was not thought of as a part of the group that migrated out of Egypt.

There has been lively debate about Dan, and one of the observations is that this tribe may have been associated with the Denyen, part of the Sea People confederacy. Excavations at Tell el-Qadi provide some information. Tell el-Qadi has been identified as the biblical city of Dan. Archaeological investigation of the site shows major signs of Aegean influence. Tell el-Qadi is now referred to as Tel Dan, and tomb evidence indicates that ceramic vessels found in the burial site originated in the Mycenaean culture. Other artifacts suggest that people who lived in this area originated somewhere in the Aegean.

One hypothesis states that the Danites were actually mercenaries hired by the Egyptians to keep order in the territory. If so, the people of Dan might have been in the region before the official Hebrew migration. To tie them back to the Hebrews, the tribe of Dan might have decided to ally themselves with the Hebrews and assimilate into the Hebrew culture.

Returning to the investigation of why Dan "abided with the ships," we can assume this was not solely a land-based group of people. Dan was located near the coast of the Mediterranean Sea and probably had a maritime presence. They may have been aware of the naval technology of the Sea People and used it.

We can only guess at Dan's role in the ongoing struggle between the Hebrews and the Philistines. One possibility is that Dan gave the Hebrews a nautical force the Hittites never had. While it might not have meant that Dan was employed in conducting raids against Sea People outposts, the tribe of Dan could have responded proactively to Sea People raids (Bohstrom, 2016).

Continued Resistance

The struggle between the Hebrews and the Philistines was not settled by one major battle, like the Egyptian victory at the Battle of the Delta. Instead, it was an ongoing conflict between two peoples that lasted for centuries. It was not until the reign of King David in the 10th century BCE that significant progress was made against these descendants of the Sea People. David defeated the Philistines in several important battles and ultimately compelled the Philistines to pay tribute to him.

The Hebrews were a stubborn opponent. Their ability to withstand outside aggression stemmed from a unified culture and religion. Hebrews considered themselves to be a chosen people, and that belief was integral to Hebrew social and cultural identity. They followed a strict set of religious laws and practices, and these rules and customs provided them with a national identity that made them tough to overcome.

Unlike the Mycenaean city-states, the Hebrews had a hinterland to which they could retreat in the event of a defeat. The Carmel range, which extends from the Mediterranean Sea to the Jezreel Valley, offered geographical protection that could be used in times of trouble. Sea People were basically inhabitants of the coastlines. They did not have sufficient knowledge to take and control mountainous areas. Although Sea People, particularly Philistines, did conduct raids into Hebrew territory, these were still hit-and-run incursions. Hebrews could retreat but then come back again. Moreover, their cultural identity and purpose made it difficult to bring their society to the ground. It would take a superior force, such as the Assyrians and Babylonians in later centuries, to inflict lasting damage on them.

The Sea People faced formidable opposition from Egypt and Canaan. These territories may have had internal disputes and attacks from other areas, but their societies were strong enough to heal and recover. The Sea People were not the mighty and invincible foe they proved to be against the Hittite Empire and the Greeks. The days of roving the waters and looking for victims were starting to fade.

Sea People may have been the victims of their own success. Once a city was razed to the ground, it would be difficult for it to come back up and present itself as a victim of a future assault. Besides, the Sea People had matured.

As mentioned, the attacks conducted during the reign of Ramesses III included families. These were women and children looking for more than just a quick profit. Migrations ultimately have an ending point when people decide they would prefer to settle down and establish roots. The Sea People were no different. Archeological evidence makes it increasingly clear that they finally decided a home on land was more important than a life on the sea.

We still need more information about the Sea People, but we know that on the Mediterranean coast of the Levant was a place they could refer to as a homeland. This area contains significant archaeological digs that show a society that valued and made their fortunes in trade rather than looting. On a stretch of land in the southern part of modern-day Israel, the sea-wandering marauders decided to dock their ships and move away from piracy.

Chapter 9 – Philistia, Land of the Sea People

Civilization can be borne upon the waves, but it is rarely cultivated on the wooden decks of a ship. Archaeologists can speculate where the Sea People came from, but that does not mean they went back home and never returned to the sea. Instead, a significant theory about the Sea People is that they were part of a diaspora that took to the water to escape famine and other dangers. They were leaving one home in search of another.

One of the new homes for these wanderers was in the southwest part of modern-day Israel, a land known to history as Philistia. Research conducted on skeletons of people who lived in the ancient city of Ashkelon shows DNA originating in southern Europe. The remains were of people who had arrived around the 12th century BCE. This fits in with the notion that there was a sudden influx of people from somewhere else (Osborne, 2019).

Egyptian records mentioned the presence of families among the Sea People at the Battle of the Delta, and those settling in Philistia may have been survivors of the defeat. Egypt went through a period of decline after the death of Ramesses III, which created an opportunity for those who were settled in Philistia. As the Egyptians fell back, the new settlers took over and established their own culture (Evian, 2023).

Why Settle in Philistia?

There are several reasons scholars believe the Peleset docked their ships and put down roots in this part of the Middle East. An obvious one is the strategic location. Philistia was on the coastal plain, making it an ideal place for trade and commerce. Several trade routes went through or close to this territory, and Philistia was conveniently located close to Egypt, Mesopotamia, and what remained of trade centers in the eastern Mediterranean.

A principal trade route was the coastal road that connected Egypt with the Levant. The trade route was also available for transporting goods such as timber and incense from the southern Arabian Peninsula to various ports along the Mediterranean Sea coast. It permitted the new settlers to be intermediaries, importing goods from Egypt and exporting them to other regions. Philistia could quickly be developed into a prominent trading hub.

Additionally, the land was fertile and could sustain a large population. The possibilities for commercial success and the ability to feed a family would be sufficient to convince anyone that their roaming days were over.

Security may also have been a motivating factor. The Late Bronze Age was a period of great turmoil where danger was always a concern. Philistia had natural defense capabilities that were appealing. The Mediterranean Sea to the west, the Carmel Mountains to the north, and Judean Hills to the east were natural fortifications that just required a few improvements to make the area relatively secure. So, it made sense to call this area home.

These new people were now referred to as Philistines, and gradual migration to their corner of the Middle East may have gone on for decades. As we've seen, the Philistines were featured prominently in the Hebrew Bible and are viewed as a primary opponent of Israel.

Philistine Commercial Significance

Philistia had five commercial centers: Gaza, Ashdod, Ashkelon, Ekron, and Gath. Trade was carried on throughout the eastern Mediterranean and included commercial relations with Cyprus, Greece, and the Aegean Islands. There is evidence of economic traffic with Philistia throughout the region.

The Philistines were more than just traders. They were skilled in a number of crafts, including metalworking, pottery, and jewelry making. It is safe to say that these people got richer through commerce than they ever did through piracy.

Their expertise in metalworking included iron-making technology, which was used to create tools and weapons. This technology was valuable and contributed to the military prowess of the Philistines. Their adeptness at iron-making also hints at a development in the region that would dramatically change history.

Philistine Culture

The Philistines became noted for their artistic and cultural achievements, which drew inspiration from the surrounding regions.

Pottery was a key form of creative expression in the Philistine culture. The Philistines used a variety of techniques to make pottery, and these included wheel-throwing and hand-building. The Philistines used these techniques to create various forms, such as bowls, jugs, and lamps.

Red and black geometric designs are distinctive features of Philistine pottery. The designs are often arranged in panels or bands, and they feature abstract motifs such as spirals, zigzags, and triangles. Figurative designs, including depictions of animals and humans, are also featured.

Painting, incising, and stamping were techniques used to decorate the pottery. Painting was most common, in which colored pigments were applied to the vessel's surface. Incising involved cutting designs into the surface of the pottery, and stamping was done with a mold or stamp.

Jewelry is something else the Philistines were noted for making. Various materials were used, including gold, silver, bronze, and semiprecious stones. Filigree was a noteworthy feature of Philistine jewelry. It involves twisting and bending thin metal wires into intricate designs, which shows highly sophisticated artistry. The Philistine filigree was usually combined with granulation and inlay techniques to create highly ornamental pieces. Animal and floral motives were standard features.

As the Philistines excelled at metalworking, they would create weapons, tools, and household objects in their shops. The decorative themes used in pottery were also found in their metalwork. Additionally, metalwork employed inlays of colored glass or stone into the surface of the metal.

Textiles were an artistic medium that showcased Philistine expertise. The Philistine weavers were renowned, and their textiles featured bold, bright colors and intricate patterns. Embroidery was included in the work.

Finally, sculpture was a primary form of artistic expression. Philistines used geometric patterns and worked in stone, wood, and bone.

It appears the Philistines were more than just fighters. They developed a culture of exquisite beauty and craftsmanship in Philistia. This is in stark contrast to the image of the Sea People that is carved into the Egyptian temples. Indeed, a high level of sophistication was evident from the work these former Sea People provided once they established themselves in their new homeland.

The existence of Philistia changes the story of the Sea People. Before, they were dismissed as a wild bunch of pirates who did nothing but destroy cities and burn crops. However, the Philistia groups of the Sea People were not simply thugs. Indeed, the art and culture of Philistia demonstrate a high level of sophistication that was absent from many of the earlier accounts of these people. Like the Vikings in the Middle Ages, the Sea People could produce objects of fantastic beauty.

A possible explanation is that once established in Philistia, the Sea People had the time and the inclination to aspire to cultural activity. They no longer had to worry about feeding their families, and the topography's security gave them a sense of safety. They also established themselves on significant trade routes in the eastern Mediterranean. As a result, they were able to produce tradable goods.

Luxury items were important trade items. Textiles and jewelry were more than basic necessities; they were the goods the neighbors wanted and were willing to bargain over. Archaeological evidence suggests that the Philistines used their new homeland as a base for commercial activity that extended hundreds of miles away from Philistia.

Philistia and Israel bickered and battled for centuries, but the Hebrews did not bring down the Philistine nation. Instead, the Assyrian army, the ultimate war machine of the Iron Age, ended the Philistine civilization. Resistance against these troops from Mesopotamia was pointless, and Assyrian retribution was notably ruthless.

Philistines Versus the Hebrews

The on-again, off-again struggle between the Philistines and the Hebrews is covered in the books of Judges, Solomon, and Kings found in the Hebrew Bible. It was a contest that did not last for years but centuries and pitted two distinct cultures against each other.

Philistines had a coastal identity with several major city-states that did business all over the eastern Mediterranean. The Hebrews were, as already related, pastoral people who lived in the hill country of Palestine. Philistines had a religion with a pantheon of gods; Hebrews had just one. The latter was a big sticking point between the two groups. The Hebrews considered the Philistines evil because they would not worship Yahweh. This antique bigotry is very apparent when reading accounts in the Hebrew Bible.

A struggle for political hegemony in the region was a significant reason for the disputes. The Philistines wanted to extend their influence beyond the coast and met stiff resistance from the Hebrews. The Philistines would gain the upper hand in early encounters, but eventually, the Hebrews were able to drive them back.

The Philistines would unite in a confederacy in times of war. References in the Hebrew Bible to the Philistines include mention of the five lords. These were the rulers of Ashdod, Gath, Ashkelon, Ekron, and Gaza. Ekron was the central city (Dailyhistory.org, 2023).

References in the Hebrew Bible

The book of Judges contains several references to the Philistines and their confrontations with the Hebrews. One particularly stands out. It is Judges 3:1-4:

"Now these are the nations which the Lord left, to test Israel by them, even as many of Israel as had not known all the wars of Canaan; only that the generations of the children of Israel might know, to teach them war, at the least such as for new nothing thereof: namely, the five lords of the Philistines, and all the Canaanites, and the Sidonians, and the Hivites that dwelt in Mount Lebanon, from Mount Baal-Hermon onto the entering in of Hamath."

The Philistines had a better understanding of warfare. 1 Samuel 4-7 tells of a major battle where the Hebrews were defeated and a significant religious treasure that was taken by the Philistines:

"When the Ark of the Lord's covenant came into the camp, all Israel raised such a great shout of the ground shook. Hearing the uproar, the Philistines asked, 'What's all this shouting in the Hebrew camp?'

When they learned that the ark of the Lord had come into the camp, the Philistines were afraid. 'May God come into the camp,' they said. 'Oh no! Nothing like this has happened before. We are doomed! Who will deliver us from the hand of these mighty gods? The other gods who struck the Egyptians with all kinds of plagues in the wilderness. Be strong, Philistines! As they have been to you. Be men, and fight!'

So the Philistines fought, and the Israelites were defeated, and every man fled to his tent. The slaughter was very great; Israel lost 30,000-foot soldiers. The ark of God was captured."

As mentioned, the story of Samson and the Philistines is perhaps the best-known episode of the two peoples in the Bible. Samson was probably a leader of the tribe of Dan, and the Hebrew Bible suggests that he had incredible strength. The text speaks of Samson's numerous encounters on the battlefield with the Philistines. His death is one of the more memorable stories of the Bible, found in Judges 16:

"Then Samson reached towards the two central pillars on which the Temple stood. Bracing himself against them, his right hand on one and his left hand on the other, Samson said, 'Let me die with the Philistines!' Then he pushed with all his might, and down came the Temple on the rulers and all the people in it. Thus he killed many more when he died than while he lived."

These passages need corroboration before they can be accepted as authentic. Nevertheless, they paint a picture of two ethnic groups struggling with each other and seeking to control territory.

As stated earlier, King David finally subdued the Philistines. The Hebrews had, by that time, gained military superiority. King David was a power to be reckoned with. Second Samuel 5:17-25 describes a significant confrontation between this king of Israel and the Philistines:

"When the Philistines heard that David had been anointed king over Israel, they went up in full force to search for him, but David heard about it and went down to the stronghold. Now the Philistines had come and spread out in the Valley of Rephaim, so David inquired of the Lord, 'Shall I go and attack the Philistines? Will you deliver them into my hands?'

The Lord answered him, 'Go, for I will surely deliver the Philistines into your hands.' So David went to Baal Perazim. He said, 'As the waters break out, the Lord has broken out against my enemies before me.' So that place was called Baal Perazim. The Philistines abandoned their idols there, and David and his men carried them off.

Once more, the Philistines came up and spread out in the Valley of Rephaim, so David inquired of the Lord, and he answered, 'Do not go straight up, but circle around behind them and attack them in front of the poplar trees. As soon as you hear the sound of marching in the tops of the poplar trees, move quickly because that will mean the Lord has gone out in front of you to strike the Philistine army.' So David did as the Lord commanded him, and he struck down the Philistines all the way from Gibeon to Gezer."

The Philistines were still in the area, but they were no longer the major threat they were before.

The Usefulness of Dan

Naval superiority helped the Sea People in earlier encounters with Mediterranean cultures. The Hebrews were essentially land-based, but the tribe of Dan was not. The Danites understood the waters. That relationship with the sea may have helped the Hebrews against the Philistines. Ships from the tribe of Dan may have been able to stop attempts to seize Hebrew territory further up the coast. We do not know if that happened, but it is interesting to speculate.

What is unfortunate about the stories in the Hebrew Bible is how the text concentrates on hostility. Both sides did fight frequently, but there were extended periods of peace where the two could interact. The Hebrews learned from the Philistines, and their commerce with the outside world improved because of exposure to Philistine nautical expertise. Hebrews learned a lot about military tactics and technology in a trial-and-error history of combat with the Philistines. The defeats and the victories made the Hebrews a more potent force than before.

Philistia and Israel bickered and battled for centuries, but the Hebrews did not bring down the Philistine nation. Instead, the Assyrian army, the ultimate war machine of the Iron Age, ended the Philistine civilization. Resistance against these troops from Mesopotamia was pointless, and Assyrian retribution was notably ruthless.

The irony is that the Assyrians attacked and ravaged Philistine cities as completely as the Sea People did to their victims centuries before. The Philistines ceased to be major players in the area after the Assyrians had leveled them.

The waning days of the Late Bronze Age saw fewer Sea People raids. Resistance to their incursions had stiffened, and fortifications erected by various cities made them more defensible. All the low-hanging fruit had been picked, and maritime aggression was no longer paying handsome dividends.

It seems that the Sea People were starting to settle down, and city dwelling was more common, as witnessed by Philistia. These people now became quiet inhabitants of the area, and except for the biblical references, little attention was paid to them in the following centuries. The sea rovers were now blending into the landscape.

One notable city may have been a stronghold for the Sea People, and it still captures our attention and imagination. It was a citadel whose ships plied the wine-dark seas. Scholars are still debating whether this municipality was a significant center and, if so, what its role was in the final days of the Sea People.

Chapter 10 – The Myths and Facts About Troy

The Victorian intelligentsia discounted the idea there ever was a city named Troy. The Trojan War was the basis for an epic poem of antiquity, *The Iliad,* but they had no doubt that Homer had an enormous imagination when he composed the rhymes. Everyone was convinced that Troy was nothing more than a heroic legend and was only suitable for late-night reading. One man disagreed.

Henrich Schliemann was an entrepreneur who was highly successful in the business world, becoming wealthy through his own efforts. He firmly believed that there was a city named Troy and that Homer was not exaggerating about it. Everyone laughed when this amateur archaeologist traveled to a northeastern part of Anatolia, near a place called Hissarlik, and organized an archaeological dig. They stopped laughing when Schliemann uncovered a fabulous treasure and announced that he had discovered the legendary city. Interestingly, Henrich Schliemann went on to find the ruins of Mycenae, another city that people dismissed as more of a fable than a fact.

Schliemann's discovery was the archaeological find of the 19th century. Later excavations discovered that Troy was not one city but several habitations built one on top of the other. Regardless, it is now accepted that he had uncovered a major population center of the Late Bronze Age. Troy interests us because it seems to have a solid connection to the Sea People.

The Trojan War in a Nutshell

The Trojan War has been the subject of countless retellings and adaptations over the centuries. It has been interpreted as a metaphor for the struggle between order and chaos, a cautionary tale about the consequences of private ambition, and a historical event that may have had a basis in reality.

However, the historical accuracy of the Trojan War remains a subject of debate among historians and archaeologists. Some scholars believe the Trojan War was an actual historical event that was embellished and mythologized over time. Others argue the story of the Trojan War is entirely mythical and has no basis in reality. Those in the latter group have to contend with the existence of a major archaeological excavation.

Homer gives a detailed account of the classical story of the war. The origin of the Trojan War was a kidnapping. A Trojan prince named Paris fell in love with Helen, the wife of King Menelaus of Sparta. So, Paris abducted Helen and took her back to Troy with him, setting off a chain of events that would lead to the Trojan War.

King Menelaus was outraged by the abduction of his wife and called upon the other Greek kings to help him recover her. A massive Greek army, led by Agamemnon, the king of Mycenae and brother of Menelaus, sailed across the Aegean Sea to lay siege to the city and demand the return of Helen.

The ensuing war lasted ten years, during which the Greeks and Trojans engaged in numerous battles and skirmishes. Heroes fought and died all over the plain in front of Troy. The war finally ended when the Greeks used a trick to infiltrate Troy. They built a giant wooden horse and left it outside the city's gates as a gift. The Trojans, believing the horse was a symbol of victory over the Greeks, brought it inside the city walls. However, Greek soldiers were hiding inside the horse. They emerged at night, opened the city gates, and let in the rest of the Greek army. The Greeks then sacked and burned the city of Troy, ending the war. Modern archaeology has the challenge of filling in the gaps and corroborating Homer's account.

There is a renewed interest in the Trojan War and a desire to continue the quest for archaeological evidence of the war and the events and social conditions surrounding it. The work is more than just verifying that the Trojan War happened.

The Late Bronze Age was a violent epoch. Two civilizations collapsed, and one was seriously threatened. Studying the Trojan War can give us a better understanding of the tensions that suddenly caused cultures that appeared remarkably stable to fall apart. The investigation includes looking into those involved in this martial drama.

Homer provides us with a list of the participants in this struggle. It is not two or three contestants but a wide assortment of city-states and countries of that time. Each would have a motivation for sending troops to the battleground. Learning more about the Trojan War will clarify what caused large groups in the region to form coalitions to destroy or defend Troy.

The Sea People were a prominent group at the time of the Trojan War, and it is safe to assume they were involved in the fighting. Therefore, it is not out of the question to suspect that they might also have been a significant reason for the conflict. A thoughtful analysis of the Trojan War and its participants, consequently, must include a discussion of the significance of the Sea People.

The Sea People and Troy

Some scholars have suggested that the Sea People may have been one of the groups that participated in the war, either as Trojans, Greeks, or allies of either side. The Trojan War took place at the same time as the Sea People were ravaging the Aegean Sea. A conflict of that magnitude would no doubt have attracted the interest of the Sea People. Homer, in Book II of *The Iliad*, gives a list of groups who were involved:

"Menelaus, Atrides, dear to Zeus, led the black-hulled ships, with 80 oarsmen to each ship, and each man was a warrior armed in bronze, a goodly and tall man; and they sailed to Troy, and with them sailed many other tribes of men. Among them came the Cretans, with their hundred ships, and men of Tenedos, and the men of the scattered islands, and the Achaians that dwelt about the sea."

Some scholars argue that the phrase "the men of the scattered islands" may refer to the Sea People, who were known for their seafaring abilities and may have come from various islands in the eastern Mediterranean.

Whose Side Were They On?

The references Homer made to those warriors who might have been Sea People do not say that all of them were allies of the Greeks. Book II also lists the allies of the Trojans who came to support the city as it came under attack:

"But who, of all the tribes, and count the names, the barbarous nations, and the rude hordes, with brazen shields, and two-edged spears, who came to Troy, their lives and property to stake?"

Who were the barbarian nations and the rude hordes? Homer is not as specific as the Egyptian chroniclers about the Sea People's names. The poet has used general terms to include the most prominent groups on either side. Modern researchers have the challenge of speculating who fought for whom. We must ponder whether the Sea People were the invaders or the defenders of Troy. Regrettably, there is a lack of conclusive evidence, but we have fragments of intelligence that can give us some useful clues. We will take a look at both sides.

• Sea People as Greeks or Greek Allies

Archaeological evidence indicates that one level of Troy, Troy VIIa, was destroyed during wartime. Excavation since 1988 shows that Troy was a large city surrounded by fields of wheat. The devastation occurred at the same time as the Sea People raids.

The Hittite archives mention a city in the general area that was called Tarusia, or Wilusa. Research shows that the people from this city spoke a language related to the Hittite language and that Wilusa was an ally of the Hittite Empire. This evidence offers the possibility that the Trojans were connected to the Hittite Empire and, consequently, would have been targeted by the Sea People, who regularly attacked Hittite allies (Chrysopoulos, 2022).

• Sarpedon and the Trojans

The connection between the Sea People and Troy can be found in one of the major characters in *The Iliad.* A valuable Trojan ally was Sarpedon, a warrior who fought bravely on the side of Troy. He is mentioned in the thick of a fight in many parts, including these lines from Book 14:

"Then, by the bold Sarpedon, on they pressed, and he, with flaming ardor in his breast, onward to conquer in the foremost fight."

Who is he leading into the fight? Sarpedon was not a Trojan, and he was leading his own troops into battle. Sarpedon reportedly came from an area in western Anatolia known as Lycia. It is a mountainous region, and it is mentioned frequently in Greek literature. The region is often associated with the city of Caria, and both are in *The Iliad.* Lycia is referred to in Hittite records as Lukka, one of the homelands of the Sea People found in the Egyptian records. In this case, Sarpedon and his troops would have been Sea People reinforcements sent to bolster the defenses of Troy (Burford, 2019).

Luwian People and the Black Sea

One argument in favor of the Sea People being Trojan or Trojan allies comes from the location of Troy. The Luwian people lived in western Anatolia, and Troy would have been in their territory. In addition, the Luwians were becoming influential in their own right and may have been attacked by Greeks who feared their might (Stack Exchange, 2022).

Yet another possibility paints the Sea People as the aggressors. But instead of working with the Greeks, the Sea People, whom we know came from the Aegean, may have had allies from the Black Sea. Those associates may have joined the assault, attacking Troy from the rear. The final destruction of the Hittite Empire may have been the reason for their participation. As a vassal state, Troy was just as vulnerable as the Hittite capital, Hattusa. The Black Sea allies may have had a bone to pick with Troy. The citadel of Priam may have been a base for attacks against Black Sea coast inhabitants, and they would have been all too ready to ally themselves with the Sea People to seek revenge (Holst, 2005).

The chaos of the Late Bronze Age required victims to put up a stiff defense if possible. The weakening of the Hittite Empire left vassal states on their own and allowed their enemies to settle a few scores. The Trojan War may have been the culmination of some old feuds in northeastern Anatolia and the Black Sea.

Which Came First?

The connection between the Sea People raids and the Trojan War is that both occurred at approximately the same time. This leads to a discussion about which came first in chronological order.

Assuming that the Trojan War came first, the human debris from the fall of Troy may have created a situation ripe for piracy. Veterans of the conflict would suddenly find themselves without a job or other source of income. These men knew how to fight and how to kill. Furthermore, they were familiar with sacking a city. They could have used the same ships that brought them to Troy to conduct raids all over the eastern Mediterranean. They would use their original homelands as naval bases.

Now, let us suppose that the Trojan War came second. This creates another interesting scenario. Troy might have been a city within the Luwian culture that had ties with Lukka, an identified source of the Sea People. It could be argued that Troy was a major center for the Sea People.

If this is true, the war was a counterattack launched by the Greek city-states. The Greeks may have decided that it was essential to destroy Troy to end the raids. They all came together in the hopes of trying to bring some form of stability to the region.

A final guess combines both. Troy was the objective of a coordinated military campaign involving many city-states against one central power. The veterans of the conflict, having destroyed a primary Sea People base, might have turned to piracy because the war was over and they needed to make a living, even if it meant looting unsuspecting cities.

All these conjectures are fun to consider, but they highlight a significant problem when discussing the Sea People: we do not have a reliable, definitive source of information about these maritime marauders. We are stuck in a situation where we have fragments of data, and that is it. Moreover, all we have is a negative story.

The emphasis on the bad news is comparable to the original descriptions of the Vikings. That was a case where most of what we initially knew came from the quills of terrified monks who portrayed the Vikings as savage barbarians who were no more than waterborne Huns. In the last few decades, we finally got a picture of the Viking culture. The rune stones and carvings of the Vikings were essential tools for interpreting their past. In comparison, we currently have little to go on with the Sea People.

The Trojan War is a real example of the instability of the Late Bronze Age. Future writers used it to warn about the consequences of greed and a desire for power. Plato discusses the Trojan War in his treatise, *The Republic.* He focuses on the moral and political themes of the story and how the war itself showed the consequences of factionalism and tribalism. Plato counters that by emphasizing the importance of cooperation and unity among individuals and groups from diverse backgrounds. He argues that a just and harmonious society requires the collaboration and mutual support of all its members. Those are admirable aspirations but, unfortunately, are not exclusive to a just society. Cooperation and unity can wander over to the dark side.

The Sea People came from diverse origins and backgrounds. Looking at each group separately, it appears they had a complex assortment of values and customs. Nevertheless, they were able to form a confederacy with a unified purpose. Unfortunately, they produced chaos and disorder instead of a harmonious society. To give those devils their due, we can say that the activity of the Sea People brought down a civilization that was no longer functioning adequately. A new age arose from the ashes.

Fortunately for civilization, the age of the Sea People was short-lived. There is not much evidence of any large-scale, organized pirate activity after 1150 BCE. It is as if the Sea People suddenly vanished. What caused the quick disappearance? It was not just one phenomenon or event that suddenly erased them from the historical record. The Sea People left the dramatic stage of history because of several developments.

Chapter 11: The Curtain Falls

The start of the 12th century BCE should have been an optimistic time for the Sea People. They were a commanding presence in the eastern Mediterranean and, despite a few setbacks, ruled the waves and held the nations in terror, wondering where the next attack would occur. However, by 1150 BCE, the story of the Sea People closed. What started as a lightning strike ended in a fizzle. What happened?

That question is still difficult to answer. We do not have any authoritative chronicle of the demise of these pirates. Instead, we must make educated guesses about what caused the Sea People to slip into the darkness of time. The following are possible reasons those who ruled the waves sank beneath them.

The Iron Age Began

A black swan in the business world refers to an unforeseen or unpredictable occurrence. It comes out of nowhere, and extreme and costly consequences result from its appearance. A significant black swan came in with the tide of history. It was not a new group of immigrants or a sudden natural catastrophe. It was iron.

This metal was the final blow to bring the Bronze Age to an end. There were instances of iron being smelted and used earlier, but with the dawn of the 12th century BCE, this substance was taking center stage and could not be replaced.

Bronze is the product of two metals: tin and copper. Both are needed, or it is impossible to create bronze. Iron stands alone. It does not need a sister metal to make durable weapons and implements. It requires a sophisticated forging process and considerable heat, but molten iron can be shaped into various tools using durable molds. Iron transformed weapon technology. Spears, swords, and other implements of war were more durable than bronze. Armies equipped with bronze weapons had little chance of success against enemies who used iron.

The introduction of iron had an impact on copper. Copper would always be used for luxury items and jewelry, but it lost its place at a strategic level. The demand for copper would reduce as the use of iron progressed. Any culture that was dependent on copper for prosperity was going to suffer.

Part of the success the Sea People enjoyed was their ability to influence the copper trade in the Late Bronze Age. This ability to control an essential mineral began to ebb as iron became the substance of choice for weaponry and tools. Copper relied on trade routes to bring the metal to those regions where there was none. Iron was a more common commodity; there were available deposits throughout the Middle East and the Mediterranean region. Local mines extracted iron and delivered it quickly to the forges. Attacks along the coast by the Sea People would have little effect on iron works located further inland. Consequently, the Sea People could no longer use their hegemony over copper as they once had (Pressbooks.nscc.ca, 2023).

New Competition

The Sea People had a significant advantage over their victims because of maritime technology. They were the best until someone else came along. At the end of the Bronze Age, a rival for dominance over the sea came from the Phoenicians.

The downfall of the Hittite Empire and the Mycenaean civilization, along with the weakening of other countries, created opportunities to be exploited. The Phoenicians stepped into a power vacuum that they exploited. They became known as the best traders in the eastern Mediterranean's commercial world and exported commodities that were in high demand, such as Tyrian purple, glass, and cedarwood. The Phoenicians gradually extended their influence to the Western Mediterranean and founded cities such as Carthage that could be used for trade and ports to resupply (DHWTY, 2019).

The Sea People had capitalized on their shipbuilding, and the Phoenicians did them one better. Phoenician ships had two primary designs. The trading ships were built with rounded hulls and curved sterns. These had a giant rectangular sail in the center that could turn to catch the wind. Additionally, a Phoenician trading vessel had an oar-like blade attached to the ship's left side for steering. Storage and crew space were near the rear of the boat on the quarterdeck. Their warships carried two sails. The front of the vessel had a forecastle to be used by bowmen or catapults. Moreover, there was a rostrum—a bronzed tip fitted to the front of the ship to ram other boats. These were technical advances over what the Sea People had (The Mariners' Museum and Park, 2023).

Superior ships meant that the Phoenicians did not have to rely on the traditional trade routes for prosperity. Instead, they could chart new waters and go beyond the Aegean Sea to seek their fortune. Instead of waiting for trading partners to come to them, the Phoenicians could sail out to the sources for goods. Phoenician ships could sail to the coast of Spain and return. Best of all, Phoenician colonies created throughout the Western Mediterranean made it convenient for the sea captains to put in at a friendly port.

The Phoenicians' ship design would allow them to outrun any Sea People raiding vessel. In addition, they were more than a match in battle for what the Sea People had. The Sea People did conduct raids against Phoenician ports, but that did not mean those cities collapsed into ruin. On the contrary, seaports such as Sidon were rebuilt quickly. The Phoenicians learned from the mistakes of others and discovered ways that the Sea People could be thwarted. Coastal fortifications were created to defend Phoenician harbors.

The Phoenicians also had a commercial advantage because of their writing system. The Phoenician alphabet helped in communication. They could enter into treaties and trade agreements with other groups. That diplomatic dexterity permitted them to gradually absorb any punishment the Sea People dished out and still keep progressing.

To sum it up, the Phoenicians were viable competitors for the Sea People. As a result, the Sea People could not bring their Phoenician competitors down. Instead, the Phoenicians gradually outperformed and outmaneuvered what was left of the organized raiding parties. They survived where others had earlier failed.

A Serious Military Threat

The Sea People faced obstacles whenever they dealt with a nation-state that had the cohesion and military power to present a realistic counter to their raids. As the Bronze Age finally collapsed, the Sea People faced a nightmare coming out of Mesopotamia and Eastern Anatolia they never experienced before: the Assyrians.

The Hittite Empire had shielded the Sea People from Assyrian aggression since the Hittites stood between them and this major power coming out of the East. However, the collapse of the Hittite Empire exposed the Sea People to a massive, threatening force.

Assyria can be described as an engine of destruction. It had greater military technology and did not hesitate to use terror tactics to seize and maintain control over large areas of the Levant. It was capable of causing significant damage to anyone who stood in its way, and the Hebrew Bible provides graphic descriptions of what Assyrians on the march were capable of doing.

The Assyrians did not tolerate any opposition, and their army was a steamroller. If that was not rough enough, Assyria also had something that other countries lacked: a navy. As a result, the Assyrians could defend their coast with a fleet of ships, and these vessels were as maneuverable as the Sea People's ships.

The Assyrians could also use diplomacy to throttle their opposition. Alliances and treaties with neighbors allowed the Assyrians to isolate the Sea People and prevent them from forming partnerships with other groups. This force out of Mesopotamia was simply too great to resist, and the Sea People were just one of the many groups who fell before Assyria.

Assimilation and Settlement

As discussed earlier, an account of the Battle of the Delta mentions that the Sea People brought their families. It is accepted that the Sea People were looking for more than just a smash and grab opportunity. They were tribes seeking a place to settle down and raise their families in security. The Egyptians settled on a policy of assimilation where Sea People tribes such as the Sherden were permitted to settle in territory controlled by Egypt. This worked where swords and spears failed.

It was easy to domesticate roving warriors. The Egyptians relocated them to areas where they would serve as buffers and permitted them to become part of the local population. Interestingly, the Egyptians taxed them just as regularly as they did any of their other subjects. This created an irony: whatever booty the Sea People looted from the Egyptians was regularly paid back to the taxman.

Troy Playing a Role?

A lot of discussion about the Trojan War continues: what caused it and what ended it. The lack of definitive texts permits people to offer possible reasons that must, of course, have corroboration. We do not assume to be experts in the Trojan War, but we think there is enough to suggest what might have happened, and our theory includes the Sea People. Moreover, we believe the Sea People had a significant role because the coinciding fall of Troy and the end of the sea raids appears to be more than just a coincidence.

We think that Troy was a critical Sea People port. Its position permitted Troy to communicate with the various Sea People tribes and groups from the Black Sea. In our humble opinion, the importance of Troy is such that if it was not the capital of the confederacy, it was the coordination center. It is possible that an annual meeting of tribal representatives determined who would be allowed to attack what areas and when. This would be comparable to several Mafia families meeting to divide the territory.

Helen might not have gone willingly at all; she may have been kidnapped in a raid and taken to Troy, where she was held until a sizable ransom could be paid. Menelaus was not only angered by the abduction of his wife but also may have been upset by the size of the ransom. His message to other Greek cities was to take the opportunity to end the Sea People problem once and for all. It explains why so many joined in the attack on Troy. Each Greek participant wanted to solve the problem permanently.

We leave the rest of the story of the Trojan War to the experts and the poets. However, we believe that Troy was so significant to the Sea People confederacy that once it fell, the communication system between tribes collapsed. The Trojan War, in our view, was the end of the confederacy, and from then on, it was every tribe for itself. It remains for future discoveries to determine if we are right or wrong.

Final Note

It may have been one reason or several that ended the sea raids. We do not know it all, and we can only speculate. There still needs to be a definitive written account, and we continue to look for an answer.

History will offer its information if we are willing to dig for it. Archaeology, especially biblical archaeology, investigates the truth underneath the surface. As a result, we know more about the Sea People than we did 150 years ago, and the search continues.

Perhaps the elusive Sea People are only a few inches underneath some of the rubble these marauders left behind. We need to look for it.

Chapter 12: A Call for Archaeology

It would be wonderful if something comparable to the library at Herculaneum were discovered to tell us all about the Sea People. Unfortunately, that has not yet happened, and investigating the evidence is not easy. The range of Sea People activity is hundreds of nautical miles and continued for more than 100 years. There are several places where evidence of the Sea People has been found, and they do shed light on these ancient pirates.

Archaeological Sites

- Greece
  - Lefkandi

    This archaeological site is located on the island of Euboea in central Greece. It was an important city during the Late Bronze Age and the Iron Age and was occupied by the Sea People.

  - Pylos

    Pylos is located on the western coast of the Peloponnese peninsula in southern Greece. It was destroyed by the Sea People in the late 12th century BCE.

  - Nichoria

    It is located in the southwestern part of the Peloponnese peninsula, and evidence shows it was occupied by the Sea

People in the late 12th century BCE.

- o Tiryns

  Located in the northeastern part of the Peloponnese peninsula, Tiryns was destroyed by the Sea People in the late 12th century BCE.

- Egypt
  - o Medinet Habu

    It is located on the West Bank of the Nile River in Luxor, Egypt. It is a temple complex built by Ramesses III, and the walls are decorated with scenes of battle with the Sea People.

  - o Tell el-Dab'a

    The excavation site is in the eastern Nile Delta of Egypt. It is where the capital Hyksos was located and may have an association with the Sea People.

- Cyprus
  - o Kition

    Kition was an ancient city located on the southern coast of Cyprus. It was an important trade center during the Late Bronze Age and has yielded pottery and metal objects associated with the Sea People. Unfortunately, it was destroyed by the Sea People in the 12th century BCE.

  - o Amathus

    It is also located in southern Cyprus and was a trade port. It, too, was devastated by the Sea People in the late 12th century BCE.

- Israel
  - o Tel Dor

    Tel Dor is located on the Mediterranean coast of Israel and was destroyed by the Sea People in the late 12th century BCE. However, the site has yielded significant findings of cultural materials identified with the Sea People.

- Turkey
  - Tell Tayinat

    It is located in southeastern Turkey and was a significant city during the Late Bronze Age. However, it was leveled to the ground by the Sea People in the 12th century BCE.

The Philistines lived along the eastern coast of the Mediterranean in the area that is now modern-day Israel and Palestine. Philistia is the main area identified with the Sea People and where members of the confederacy put down roots. Several archaeological sites have produced significant artifacts.

- Ashdod

  This is one of the five Philistine cities mentioned in the Hebrew Bible. It was a significant trading center.

- Ekron

  Some scholars claim this is the principal city of the Philistines. It is in the Shepalah region of Israel.

- Tell el-Farah

  It is an archaeological site in the northern Jordan Valley of Palestine. The Philistines occupied it during the Iron Age. Although that is a time after the heyday of the Sea People, it might provide information about how they settled down and created a sustainable culture.

Other sites that may hold information about the Sea People include Hattusa and Tell Qasile.

What Evidence Is Important

It appears that almost all the information we have about the Sea People involves conflict. This tells us how aggressive they were, but we need more insights into this mysterious confederacy. It is important to continue uncovering material that shows the destructive nature of the Sea People, but there are other bits of information defined in the excavations.

Scholars believe that the presence of the Sea People in the eastern Mediterranean region resulted from significant migration brought on by war, famine, or considerable climate change. We can seek evidence of migration, such as changes in settlement patterns, evidence of cultural exchange and mixing, and new settlements that are discovered in areas previously uninhabited.

The current understanding of Sea People is limited. However, they did use tools, weapons, and ceramics similar to those used by other groups during the Late Bronze Age. Therefore, archaeologists can look for these artifacts and determine if a distinctive style or motif can be associated with the Sea People.

Skeletal remains hold some significant clues to more than just physical characteristics or lifestyle. Skeletons contain traces of DNA. By comparing DNA samples with skeletal remains found elsewhere, we might better understand where the Sea People originated.

We Need a Rosetta Stone

The translation of the Rosetta Stone finally allowed us to look into the depths of Egyptian history. We need something comparable to find out more about the Sea People. Researchers have hinted that the Luwian language may have been the lingua franca of the Sea People and may be the key to unlocking this mystery.

Recently, there was great excitement about a 29-meter-long Luwian inscription from the Late Bronze Age, originally found in Beykoy, Turkey, which was supposedly deciphered. Scholars hoped this would be the Rosetta Stone of the Sea People. Regrettably, this inscription has been proven to be a forgery. Furthermore, the scholar who created this fraud had been fabricating inscriptions for years (The History Blog, 2018).

This was not the first time forgery has been used in antiquity studies. Researchers need to be on their guard to avoid being duped by the work of a skillful liar. Nevertheless, there is a definite possibility that the Luwian language is the gateway to knowledge about the Sea People. It is still a fascinating prospect.

Suppose we find a way to interpret the Luwian text and discover a trove of information about the Sea People. In that case, we must be ready to accept that newly-translated inscriptions will turn our view of the Sea People upside down.

This is what happened in the case of the Maya. Archaeologists once concluded that the Mayans were a collection of stargazers who lived a peaceful existence in Mesoamerica. However, Mayan hieroglyphs are now being translated, and the new picture is a shocker. These were not peaceful farmers; they were rather aggressive warriors who were looking at the stars at night and battling each other during the day.

We may eventually find that the Sea People's real motivations had little to do with what we imagine. This does not necessarily mean that they wrote elaborate poems or created breathtaking works of art. But it would mean that they might have been more sophisticated than they had initially been given credit.

Archaeology is primarily the art of learning ancient truths, and biblical archaeology is particularly helpful. We may question some of the passages of the Hebrew Bible in regard to the history of the era. However, this text has been a reliable source for uncovering the location of many historical sites. It continues to be a helpful tool.

Sea People are still a mystery, but that might not be a permanent state of affairs. Therefore, archaeological research in the eastern Mediterranean needs to be encouraged. Hopefully, there will be a day when we uncover the full story of the Sea People and their culture. Then, we can expect to be completely amazed.

Conclusion

There is an exciting concept found in management science. It is called creative chaos. It postulates that there is a free flow of ideas and experimentation in an environment of ambiguity, uncertainty, and unpredictability. Chaos theory further points out that chaotic systems can exhibit destructive and creative tendencies. It all depends on how they are managed. There can be good or bad outcomes.

The image of the Sea People often looks like a society with attention-deficit hyperactivity disorder: they appear to be impulsive and have a total lack of restraint. That is a negative image that is not always fair, in our opinion.

The Sea People were part of the Late Bronze Age, a period of instability brought on by numerous factors. Chaos was everywhere, even where the Sea People were not roving. Climate change and natural disasters brought about unpredictability as much as a pirate ship on the waters. But something came out of the chaos.

New trade routes sprang up from the debris of the old ones. Major cities were indeed decimated and flattened, but new ones rose in their place. The best example is Troy, which had several layers of civilization after the Trojan War. The Mycenaean civilization came crashing to the ground, but Phoenician culture started to bloom as this commercial rival collapsed.

We can think of the Sea People as destructive demons from hell, and we can also view them as agents of change. Some civilizations, such as the Hittite Empire, were tottering before the first raid took place. Those societies continued to survive only because there was nothing to take them down. But, as we said earlier, the Sea People kicked in the already-rotten door.

We have much to learn from the Sea People era. One example is how to manage a diaspora. Sea People migrations caused by climate change were met by various responses. It seems that the Egyptian policy of assimilation may have been very beneficial.

The Sea People held an advantage because they used new maritime technology. The Phoenicians improved on that knowledge and produced even better ships. Could the Phoenicians have been successful if the old Hittite Empire was still around? We do not know.

We can debate whether history repeats itself. What we ought to keep in mind is that history is one of the most outstanding teachers. We learn from the experiences of others and how earlier generations met new challenges. Currently, we face numerous threats to the civilized order, including climate change and migrations of large groups. Perhaps if we learn more about the Sea People, we can find better ways to resolve these problems. We might also better understand how what appears to be chaos is actually a creative process that brings about significant, positive change.

Here's another book by Captivating History that you might like

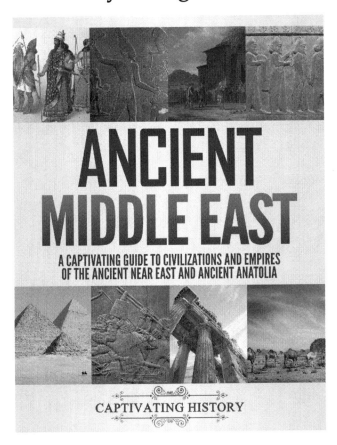

Free Bonus from Captivating History (Available for a Limited time)

Hi History Lovers!

Now you have a chance to join our exclusive history list so you can get your first history ebook for free as well as discounts and a potential to get more history books for free! Simply visit the link below to join.

Captivatinghistory.com/ebook

Also, make sure to follow us on Facebook, Twitter and Youtube by searching for Captivating History.

Bibliography

Ancient Near East. (2023, May 30). *Jaffa-Tel Aviv*. Retrieved from Ancientneareast.tripod.com: https://ancientneareast.tripod.com/Jaffa_Yafo_Aviv.html

Ancient-origins.net. (2015, May 25). *The Battle of the Delta: Ramesses III saves Egypr from the People of the Sea.* Retrieved from Ancient-origins.net: https://www.ancient-origins.net/history-important-events/battle-delta-ramses-iii-saves-egypt-people-sea-003119

Anderson, R. (2023, April 14). *Touregypt. net.* Retrieved from Who Were teh Sea People: http://www.touregypt.net/featurestories/seapeople.htm

Associates for Biblical Research. (2006, March). *The Shiloh Excavations.* Retrieved from Biblearchaeology.org: https://biblearchaeology.org/research/patriarchal-era/3640-the-genesis-philistines

Beckman, G. (2023, April 10). *Akkadian and the Hittites.* Retrieved from Brill.com: https://brill.com/display/book/edcoll/9789004445215/BP000025.xml

Biblical Historial Context. (2023, April 30). *Israelite Origins: The Late Bronze Age.* Retrieved from Biblicalhistoricalcontext.com: https://biblicalhistoricalcontext.com/israelite-origins/israelite-origins-the-late-bronze-age-collapse/

Bohston, P. (2016, December 4). *Tribe of Dan: Sons of Israel, or of Greek Mercenaries Hired by Egypt?* Retrieved from Haaretz.com: https://www.haaretz.com/archaeology/2016-12-04/ty-article-magazine/tribe-of-dan-sons-of-israel-or-of-greek-mercenaries-hired-by-egypt/0000017f-f2fa-d497-a1ff-f2fac60a0000

Bohstrom, P. (2016, December 4). *The Tribe of Dan: Sons of Israel, or of Greek Mercenaries Hired by Egypt?* Retrieved from Haaretz.com: https://www.haaretz.com/archaeology/2016-12-04/ty-article-magazine/tribe-of-dan-sons-of-israel-or-of-greek-mercenaries-hired-by-egypt/0000017f-f2fa-d497-a1ff-f2fac60a0000

Burford, F. (2019, April 25). *Lycia: Mysterious Sea Peoples of Ancient Southwest Anatolia.* Retrieved from Brewminate.com: https://brewminate.com/lycia-mysterious-sea-peoples-of-ancient-southwest-anatolia/

Chrysopoulos, P. (2022, June 25). *The Trojan:History or Myth.* Retrieved from Greekreporter.com: https://greekreporter.com/2022/06/25/trojan-war/

Cleopatra Egypt Tours. (2023, April 28). *Cleopatraegypttours.com.* Retrieved from The Battle of the Delta (Djahy): https://www.cleopatraegypttours.com/travel-guide/ancient-egypt-battles/battle-of-the-delta-1175-bc/

Cline, E. (2016, September). *Ask a Near Eastern Professional: Who are the Sea Peoples and what role did they play in the devastation of civiliztions that occurred shortly after 1200 BCE?* Retrieved from Asor.org: https://www.asor.org/anetoday/2016/09/who-sea-peoples/

Dailyhistory.org. (2023, April 30). *Who Were The Philistines and Israelites Enemies.* Retrieved from Dailyhistory.org: https://dailyhistory.org/Why_Were_the_Philistines_and_Israelites_Enemies

David Kaniewski, E. V. (2011, June 8). *The Sea Peoples, from Cuneiform Tablets to Carbon Dating.* Retrieved from Journaks.plos.org: https://journals.plos.org/plosone/article?id=10.1371/journal.pone.0020232

DHWTY. (2019, June 10). *The Phoenicians: Mysterious Merchant Mariners Whose Inventions Impacted the World Forever.* Retrieved from Ancient-Origins.net: https://www.ancient-origins.net/history-famous-people/phoenicians-0012120

Doherty, G. (2022, June 7). *Death from the Waves-the Sea People.* Retrieved from Gordondoherty.co.uk: https://www.gordondoherty.co.uk/writeblog/death-from-the-waves-the-sea-people

Editors, H. (2019, September 19). *Mycenae.* Retrieved from History.com: https://www.history.com/topics/ancient-greece/mycenae

Emanuel, J. P. (2014, December 1). *Sea Peoples, Egypt,and the Aegean: The Transference of Maritime Technology oin the Late Bronze-Early Iron Transition (LH IIIB-C.* Retrieved from Aegeussociety.org: https://www.aegeussociety.org/wp-content/uploads/2017/10/Aegean-Studies-vol1-2-Emanuel.pdf

Evian, D. S.-D. (2023, April 30). *The Philistines:Ancient Records,*

Archaeological Remains, and Biblical Traditions. Retrieved from Thetorah.com: https://www.thetorah.com/article/the-philistines-ancient-records-archaeological-remains-and-biblical-traditions

Futile World. (2021, April 3). *The Sea Peoples.* Retrieved from Futileworld.com: https://futileworld.com/2021/04/03/the-sea-peoples-tyre/

Hemingway, C. H. (2004, October). *Cyprus-Land of Copper.* Retrieved from Metmuseum.org: https://www.metmuseum.org/toah/hd/cyco/hd_cyco.htm

History Files. (2023, Apri; 12). *historyfiles.co.uk.* Retrieved from Near East Kingdoms: Anatolia: https://www.historyfiles.co.uk/KingListsMiddEast/AnatoliaLukka.htm

Holst, S. (2005, June 28). *Sea Peoples and the Phoenicians: A Critical Turning Point in History.* Retrieved from Phoenician.org: https://phoenician.org/sea_peoples/

Lacey, T. (2022, July 19). *The Merneptah Stele.* Retrieved from Answersingenesis.org: https://answersingenesis.org/archaeology/merneptah-stele/

Luwian Studies. (2023, Apri; 11). *The Initial Sea Peoples Raids.* Retrieved from Luwianstudies.org: https://luwianstudies.org/the-initial-sea-peoples-raids/

Luwian Studies. (2023, April 14). *The Sea Peoples' Inscription and Excavation Results.* Retrieved from Luwianstudies.org: https://luwianstudies.org/the-sea-peoples-inscriptions-and-excavation-results/

Millek, J. (2022, December). *Asor.org.* Retrieved from The Fall of the Bronze Age and the Destruction that Wasn't: https://www.asor.org/anetoday/2022/12/fall-bronze-age/

Milligan, M. (2020, October 9). *Who Were the Sea People.* Retrieved from HeritageDaily: https://www.heritagedaily.com/2020/10/who-were-the-sea-people/135782

O'Reilly, F. (2022, April 12). *What Caused the Collapse of the Legendary Bronze Age?* Retrieved from Retrospectjournal.com: https://retrospectjournal.com/2022/12/04/what-caused-the-collapse-of-the-legendary-bronze-age/

Osborne, H. (2019, July 3). *Biblical Philistines and the 'Sea Peoples': Ancient Dna Is Starting to Reveal Who These Mystery People Were.* Retrieved from Newsweek.com: https://www.newsweek.com/biblical-philistines-sea-peoples-dna-1447114

Pressbooks.nscc.ca. (2023, April 30). Retrieved from Chapter 3: The Bronze Age And The Iron Age: https://pressbooks.nscc.ca/worldhistory/chapter/chapter-3-the-bronze-age-and-the-iron-age/

Schiavo, S. S. (2020, May 13). *Late Bronze Age Metal Exploitationand Trade: Sardinia and Cyprus.* Retrieved from Tandfonline.com: https://www.tandfonline.com/doi/full/10.1080/10426914.2020.1758329

Stack Exchange. (2022, August). *Is there a link between the Sea people and the Trojan War?* Retrieved from History.stackexchange,com: https://history.stackexchange.com/questions/23588/is-there-a-link-between-the-sea-people-and-the-trojan-war

Tamara Stech Wheeler, R. M. (2023, April 26). *Ingots and the Bronze Age Copper Trade in the Mediterranean A Progress Report.* Retrieved from Penn.musuem: https://www.penn.museum/sites/expedition/ingots-and-the-bronze-age-copper-trade-in-the-mediterranean/

The History Blog. (2018, March 12). *Famed archaeologist forged murals, inscriptions for decades.* Retrieved from Thehistoryblog.com: https://www.thehistoryblog.com/archives/50869

The Mariners' Museum and Park. (2023, May 1). *Phoenician Ships.* Retrieved from Exploration.marinersmuseum.org: https://exploration.marinersmuseum.org/watercraft/phoenician-ships/

The Univesity of Chicago Press Journals. (2023, April 12). *New Evidence from Dor for the First Appearance of the Phoenicians along the Northern Coast of Israel.* Retrieved from Jounrals.uchicago.edu: https://www.journals.uchicago.edu/doi/10.2307/1357206

Tigue, K. (2023, February 10). *Scientists Say Climate Change Contributed to the Bronze Age Collapse-One of History's Biggest Riddles.* Retrieved from Insideclimatenews.org: https://insideclimatenews.org/news/10022023/scientists-say-climate-change-contributed-to-the-bronze-age-collapse-one-of-historys-biggest-riddles/

TimeMaps. (2023, April 10). *The Hittites.* Retrieved from TimeMaps.com: https://timemaps.com/civilizations/the-hittites/

Tornos News. (2018, October 4). *New study finds: Ancient Mycenaean civilization might have collapsed due to uprising or invasion.* Retrieved from Tornosnews.gr: https://www.tornosnews.gr/en/greek-news/culture/30911-new-study-mycenaean-civilization-might-have-collapsed-due-to-uprising-or-invasion.html

University of Gothenburg. (2023, March 26). *How Copper Deposits Turned a Village Into One of the Most Important Trade Hubs of the Late Bronze Age.* Retrieved from Scitechdaily.com: https://scitechdaily.com/how-copper-deposits-turned-a-village-into-one-of-the-most-important-trade-hubs-of-the-late-bronze-age/

Vuckovic, A. (2020, June 24). *Ancient-origins.net.* Retrieved from Ancient Egyptian Wars-Navigating the Millennia of Bloodshed: https://www.ancient-origins.net/ancient-places-africa/ancient-egyptian-wars-0013894

Wikipedia.org. (2023, April 28). *Battle of the Delta.* Retrieved from Wikipedia.org: https://en.wikipedia.org/wiki/Battle_of_the_Delta

Wikipedia.org. (2023, April 30). *Merneptah.* Retrieved from Wikipedia.org: https://en.wikipedia.org/wiki/Merneptah

Wikipedia.org. (2023, April 16). *Nuragic Civilization.* Retrieved from Wikipedia.org: https://en.wikipedia.org/wiki/Nuragic_civilization

Wikipedia.org. (2023, April 14). *Sea Peoples.* Retrieved from Wikipedia.org: https://en.wikipedia.org/wiki/Sea_Peoples

Zion, I. B. (2014, February 13). *Roving Sea Peoples may have settled Transjordan, archaeologist says.* Retrieved from The Times of Israel.com: https://www.timesofisrael.com/roving-sea-peoples-may-have-settled-transjordan-archaeologist-says/

Made in the USA
Middletown, DE
09 August 2024

58853775R00060